A World of Wheels

Cars of the Thirties

A WORLD OF WHEELS

The Dawn of Automation, Painless Sophistication and the Rice of Bright Colours

Michael Sedgwick

MASON CREST PUBLISHERS, INC.

A World of Wheels - **Cars of the Thirties**

World copyright © 2002
Nordbok International,
P.O. 7095, SE 402 32 Gothenburg, Sweden

This edition is published in 2002 by Mason Crest Publishers Inc.
370 Reed Road, Broomall, PA 19008, USA
(866) MCP-BOOK (toll free).
www.masoncrest.com

Cover: Bengt Ason Holm

First printing
1 2 3 4 5 6 7 8 9 10
Library of Congress Cataloging-in-Publication Data on file at the Library of Congress

ISBN 1-59084-484-X

Printed & bound in The Hashemite Kingdom of Jordan 2002

CONTENTS

1

THE HERITAGE OF THE TWENTIES

The 1930s have been summarized as "the age of planned obsolescence and pure transportation".

This is a facile summary which will not bear too close a scrutiny. Planned obsolescence was certainly implicit in the whole cycle of the mass-produced automobile, whose expectation of life decreased from eight or nine years to about six by 1939. Development, however, marched far more slowly in the inter-war period; if, in 1914, a 1900 Benz would have been totally unsuited for everyday motoring, there were, in 1939, probably more than two million Model T Fords of 1927 and earlier vintage still in daily use, not to mention comparable numbers of 501 Fiats, 5CV Citroëns, and Austin Twelves from the same period. Those who slate the expendability of the 1930s automobile should also consider that force of circumstances condemned it to a prolonged existence comparable to that of Jonathan Swift's Struldbrugs. Outside the United States sound 1939 models still had a modest transportation-value twenty years later, while in countries with inadequate industries and heavy import restrictions – East Germany, for instance, or New Zealand – they were condemned to soldier on far longer. A 1939 Chevrolet Master coupé encountered by the writer on an Auckland used-car lot in 1964 had depreciated no more than twenty per cent in a quarter of a century!

As for the role of "pure transportation", this had long been assumed in the United States, where the industry's first million year had been in 1916. In the last pre-Depression season of 1929, America's factories had turned out 4.5 million units. In 1930, $600 (£120) bought a new Ford Fordor sedan; the customer who preferred the smoothness of six cylinders could have them on a Chevrolet for another $75. If Britain and France still lagged behind, either country had an annual potential of a cool 250,000 units; further, they could sell these at prices accessible to the middle class, if not as yet to workers, whose weekly pay packets seldom exceeded $25 (£5).

Nor is it fair to say that the Great Depression placed a major brake on the spread of the automobile. In the matter of new-car sales, it certainly did; Morris's deliveries fell from 63,522 in 1929 to 43,582 in 1931, and Fiat's even more dramatically from 42,780 to 16,419. Chevrolet, whose first million year had been 1927, were down to barely 300,000 in the dark atmosphere of 1932. The slump had, however, less effect on actual ownership; wherever possible, motorists either hung on to their existing vehicles or bought secondhand. This state of affairs was clearly reflected in the United States, where a seventy-five per cent drop in new registrations was balanced by a fall of only ten per cent in licences issued.

In fact, 1929's stock market crash would serve as a spur to the industry; in order to stay in business, manufacturers had to provide more for less money. Purists might lament the cheese-paring influence of the cost accountant, but retail prices fell steadily from 1930 to 1938's "little recession", when a cut-back in demand was compensated by the loss of production necessitated by the exigencies of rearmament in most countries. Already, shop capacity was being redeployed to meet the requirements of the fighting services, with "shadow factories" being set up in Britain and Germany, and even the Americans questing additional sources of aero engines.

Britain and the United States, with their relatively stable economies, offer perhaps the best yardsticks. At the beginning of our decade, the Chevrolet Six offered mechanical brakes, a beam axle at either end, a "crash" gearbox calling for double-clutch techniques, and fixed disc wheels on which only the rims were demountable. Its 1936 counterpart cost £20 ($100) less, yet the brakes had been given hydraulic actuation, the front wheels were independently sprung, all wheels were demountable, and the presence of synchromesh on the two upper gear ratios made for painless shifting. Better still, wood had virtually been eliminated from the body structure, even if the price of freedom from rot and distortion was drumming at high speeds. The 1930 Morris Minor sedan, priced at £130 ($650), had indifferent stopping power, an overhead camshaft motor which offered considerable performance potential at the cost of complicated maintenance, and most of the other 1920s characteristics encountered on the Chevrolet, the demountable rims apart. Yet, for a couple of pounds more in 1936, the British motorist was offered the immortal Series I Eight, hydraulics, sliding roof, and all. It was, admittedly, a pedestrian side-valve, but its servicing needs were minimal, and it was 5 mph (8 km/h) faster than any stock Minor.

One paid, of course, in terms of individuality. The Chevrolet looked like most other American cars, down to the fashionable fencer's-mask grille on which the bow-tie badge survived as identification. Facias were now designed by stylists rather than engineers; while the home mechanic still enjoyed the convenience of a sideways-opening hood, he would not enjoy it much longer. The alligator type with its fixed sides was on the way. The Morris might adhere more closely to the traditional idiom, but its sedan bodywork was a direct crib of the 1932 Model Y Ford (and thus of the contemporary V8 from Dearborn), the curious wasp-waisted dashboard with its postage-stamp size instruments was hardly a delight, and the "honeycomb" radiator was strictly a dummy, concealing a cheap tubular affair a few inches further aft.

Fiat evolution, 1919–30. (*Top left*) A 501 roadster of the type made from 1919 to 1926, (*bottom*) a complete car and a chassis of the 990-cc 509 family spanning the years 1925–29, and (*top right*) the six-cylinder 521, the company's regular big-medium type from 1928 to 1931. This is by no means even a partial model sequence, for though the 501 ran to 1.5 litres (a favoured size in Europe), the 509 was almost a true baby, even if its 102-in (2.6 m) wheel-base allowed plenty of room for four people, and with a 22-hp over-head-camshaft engine, it was more under-geared than under-powered. Top speed was a round 50 mph (80 km/h), whereas 45 mph (72 km/h) was the 501's comfortable limit. As a general provider to the Old World, with steady sales in countries from Norway to Spain, Fiat could not afford a mistake. And in 1928, it seemed sensible to pursue the medium-six market with the American-looking 2.5-litre 521, even if up to now Giovanni Agnelli had been reluctant to take on the massed battalions of Detroit.

After twenty years of quality cars, he was not immediately ready to attack the mass market. The 501 sold eighty thousand units in 7½ years, but it was never cheap: even in 1925, a Briton paid the price of two Morris-Cowleys, and it wasn't by any means all import duty. The car sold on the strength of its uncannily smooth and indestructible side-valve motor, giving a modest 24–27 hp. Front-wheel brakes would not be added until 1924, ignition was by magneto, and both steering wheel and gearshift were on the right. Central shift (but not left-hand drive) arrived on the 509, as did excellent

coupled four-wheel brakes. At the same time, Fiat, like most other Italian makers, opted for a Rolls-Royce shape of radiator instead of the "pear" which they'd initiated (and seen widely copied) way back in 1911. By contrast, the 521 was purest American, its four-speed transmission apart. It looked like a De Soto or Plymouth, wheels were disc or wire, a coil replaced the magneto, and left-hand drive was standard. Output was 50 hp, and the 521 managed to sell nearly twenty-three thousand units in four seasons. The company would persist hopefully with American-type flathead sixes until 1936, but despite a wide choice of wheel-base, tune, and body style, many Europeans preferred to buy American or opt for something smaller. The 522 (and its long wheel-base companion, the 524) replaced the 521 during 1931, but a three-year run barely attracted ten thousand buyers, despite the attraction of hydraulic brakes, and the final 527s (1934–36) accounted for precisely 260.

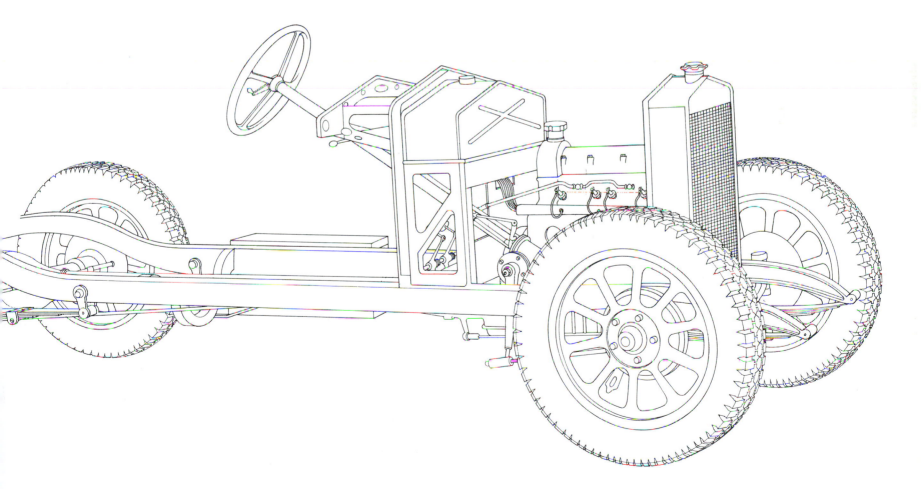

The 1920 Stutz, in some ways atypical of its country and period, has an entirely typical side-opening, two-piece hood. The advantages are immediate accessibility to, and plenty of room to work with, any part of the motor. However, one could only work on one side at a time, the catches were awkward, and the hood was heavy.

One-piece hoods (*opposite*) were one of the refinements of the thirties. The use of a dash-mounted radiator on the 1936 Fiat 500 (*top right*) ruled out underhood battery stowage and gave a short sloping nose which swung forward and could be lifted off. (It also had to be removed to insert the starting handle, an infernal nuisance when one stalled in traffic with a flat battery.) The German Ford Eifel, in 1937 form (*bottom*), offered almost equally good accessibility thanks to traditional un-streamlined fenders and deep hood sides, while rearward opening was safe enough so long as the catches held. On the 1940 Chevrolet (*top left*), however, the "alligator" hood took on its standard form for years to come and reveals its inherent failings. The fender line has now swept up to cylinder-head level, and lateral accessibility is tricky for the short-armed. Getting at anything below spark-plug level isn't easy with the normal tool kit.

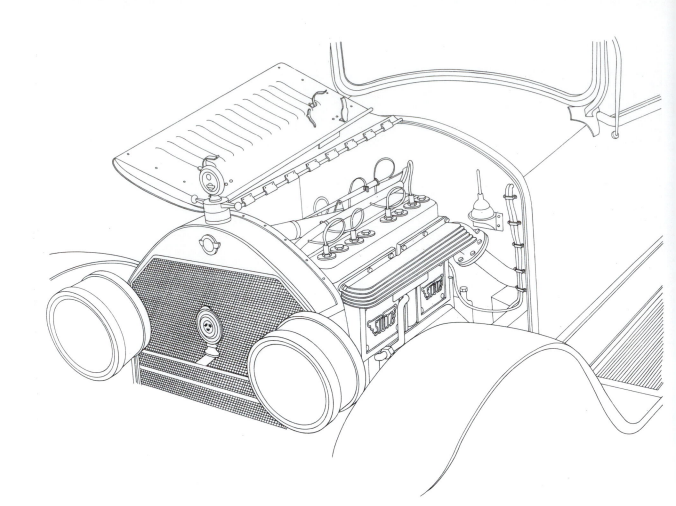

The Chevrolet and the Morris – and parallel efforts such as the 8CV Citroën, the 1.2-litre Opel, and the Fiat 508 – were, admittedly, by-products of the Depression. They signalized, however, the acceleration of a process that had gathered momentum in the previous decade as mass-production techniques spread across the Atlantic.

The advance was gradual. One may doubt if any European maker of the 1920s had a genuine potential of 100,000 units a year, and even in 1939, the ranks of the six-figure firms were probably limited to Austin, Citroën, Fiat, Morris, and Opel. But the ingredients were there; the moving assembly line, general practice in the United States by 1917–18, dominated the European cheap-car scene thirteen years later. Hot on the heels of Ford, Chevrolet, and Willys-Overland had come the redoubtable André Citroën in 1919. Morris had moved into the big league by 1924, and so had Opel in Germany with their copy of Citroën's 5CV. Fiat's first cheap baby, the 509, appeared in 1925. Edward G. Budd's all-steel closed bodies had been a reality in the United States by the 1918 Armistice, and within a decade, his methods would find footholds in Britain (the Morris-sponsored Pressed Steel Company) and in Germany (Ambi-Budd of Berlin). In France, Citroën had been making *tout acier* sedans since 1924.

Along with new, sophisticated means of manufacture had come a serious campaign to tailor the automobile to the needs of the laity. The First World War had opened the Old World's eyes to the internal combustion engine and had bred a new generation of drivers – from both sexes. These recruits might as yet be unable to afford their own transportation, but all the ingenuity of Agnelli, Ford, Morris, Opel, and the rest would have been of no avail had the end-product remained complicated and capricious, as it still tended to be in 1914.

It has been said of the "Edwardians" that they made the automobile work perfectly. This they did, but the issue has been confused by the vast depreciation of money since those days. Seen through the eyes of the 1970s, a complete Rolls-Royce Silver Ghost touring car at £1,500 (say $7,500) seems a sensational bargain – it is too easy to forget that this probably represents about £60,000 ($120,000) in present-day currency. It is even easier to discount the truth: only a tiny fraction of the day's motorists could have afforded cars of the calibre of the Royce, the bigger Mercedes, or American giants like the Pierce-Arrow and the Locomobile 48.

Further, this "perfection" of running was available only to a good driver backed by a good mechanic. Most big thoroughbreds of the day were capable of 70 mph (110 km/h), if not over-bodied, while high gearing assured a reasonable thirst – for all its 7.4-litre motor the Silver Ghost would average 16 mpg (14.5 lit/100). One had learnt to take electric lighting for granted at these exalted levels, and even outside the United States electric starters were in fairly general use. Also in evidence – albeit in Europe only – was the quick-detachable wheel, though American makers considered this too unwieldy for the distaff side and would cling obstinately to fixed wheels and demountable rims right up to 1931. Further, wheel-changes were a pressing problem, for narrow-section tyres running at high pressures on rough surfaces had a hard life, and 2,000 miles (say 3,000 km) were considered a reasonable distance for a cover. The standard source of ignition was the high-tension magneto, a contraption beyond the understanding of the average layman.

Engines still turned slowly, with narrow rev ranges. The average touring unit of 1914 idled at 400–500 rpm and was eating its guts out at 1,600. Even the big Vauxhall, a high-speed unit by the standards of the day, was doing just that speed at 60 mph (100 km/h) in high gear. Hence, few family tourers of the period were blessed with measurable acceleration, the indirect gears being regarded as emergency adjuncts

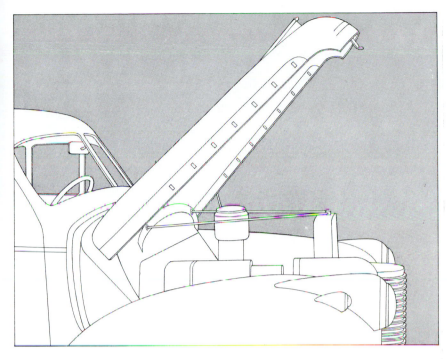

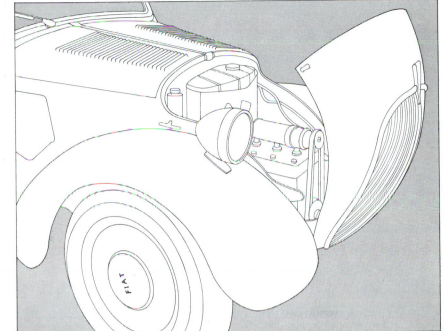

for hills or heavy city traffic. The tendency to "hang on" to top played havoc with early clutches. Progress during the 1920s can be shown by comparing Fiat's cheap 1.8-litre Zero of 1912–14 with the 990-cc 509 made in the 1925–29 period. The older car delivered its 19 brake horses at a round 1,800 rpm, whereas the 509 gave 22 bhp at a 3,400 rpm that would have horrified an Edwardian motorist. He would also have been horrified by the fierce buzzing noises emitted at 50 mph, but then he, unlike his 1929 counterpart, had no interest in the traffic-light Grand Prix.

The old Fiat Zero was capable of a respectable 45 mph (75 km/h), but even at these modest velocities, its owner had even worse problems than the limitations of early electrics or poor roads. It was far worse for the conductor of a Prince Henry Vauxhall or an Alfonso Hispano-Suiza. Even in the 1950s, such cars were physically capable of keeping up with modern traffic; what they could not do was stop in a hurry, for their two-wheel brakes called for intelligent anticipation at speeds of 60 mph or more. Little better was the foot-operated transmission brake, which produced either a rude smell or retardation on a dramatic scale, followed by side-slip and interesting consequences to the drive line.

The best hand-built coachwork of the period was superbly executed but almost invariably open; closed styles were confined to formal limousines and "doctor's coupés" (two-passenger cabriolets with winding windows and rumble seats). The traditional paint-and-varnish finish gave great depth of colour; it also required regular cleaning and renewal, if it were to retain its pristine glory. Brightwork, in brass or nickel, was quick to tarnish and the bane of a chauffeur's life.

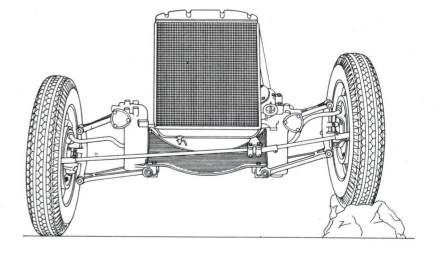

(*Top*) Belgian decline. Making luxury cars, mainly for export to Britain, didn't pay in the depressed 1930s. In 1925, however, Minerva of Antwerp had been riding the crest of the wave, with beauties like this 6-litre sleeve-valve six with coachwork by Erdmann & Rossi of Berlin. But most Minervas carried formal limousine coachwork, so sales slowly dwindled until the company was forced to amalgamate with Imperia in 1936.

The front end of 1937's Fiat 508C (*bottom*). No publicity man could resist the posed shot on a boulder to show how the coils and swinging arms kept the chassis horizontal. The Fiat handled beautifully (if one were careful with tyre pressures), but those coils in their oil-filled dashpots could freeze in sub-zero weather, with most interesting consequences!

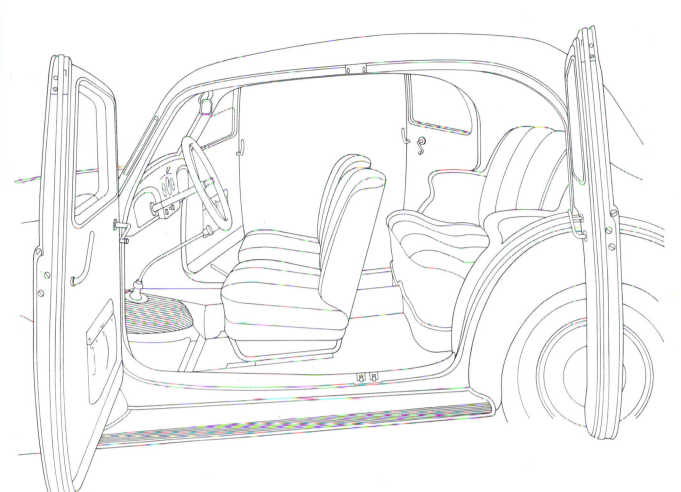

In Italian, *balilla* means "plucky little one": most people today have forgotten the association with Fascist youth movements! Of the two 508 Fiats shown here, only the 1932–33 three-speed 508 (*bottom*) is a Balilla, though the name was often applied to early 508C *Millecentos* as made between 1937 and 1952. The original Balilla was a boxy little car with a lot of 1929 De Soto in its styling. One didn't expect synchromesh on a cheap baby in 1932, and its gravity feed from a dash-mounted fuel tank would never be allowed in our safety-conscious times, and on 995 cc and 20 hp, 60 mph (95–100 km/h) were possible only downhill – until first the backyard tuners and then the factory laid hands on the car, transforming it into the delightful 36-hp 508 S sports two-seater with overhead valves. But the Balilla's short-stroke engine was unburstable – maximum power was nominally developed at 3,400 rpm, but 4,000 were entirely safe. Later four-speeders with synchromesh (1934) carried the story through to 1937, and Balillas were built under licence in France (Simca), Germany (NSU), Czechoslovakia (Walter), and even, briefly, in Spain.

The Fiat 508 C of 1937 had easy all-round access for four on a wheel-base of only 95 in (2.4 m), as this illustration (*left*) shows. Luggage lived behind the rear seat: the space wasn't shared by the spare wheel but was only accessible from inside. Unfortunately, the pillarless doors soon distorted, and then rattles and draughts were the order of the day. Fiat even applied the pillarless principle to a long-chassis six-seater edition (wheel-base was 108 in or 2.7 m) which became popular as a taxi. Unusually for a long and narrow car, it handled as well as the short model, only, with an abbreviated hood, one had to remember that most of the vehicle was behind one!

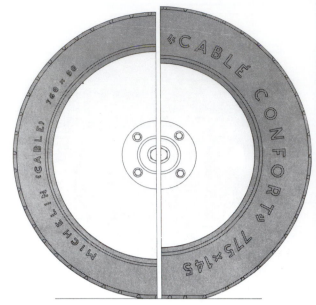

Tyre development. The sectional drawing (*above*) shows the difference between the early low-pressure type and the "balloon", first seen in 1923. The distance from axle to ground is the same in both cases, owing to the greater deflection of the modern version, which is on the right. Significantly, the low-pressure tyre, which was not new — Palmer had made "giant" tyres for formal carriages before the First World War — was offered in early days with the beaded edge, though Dunlop had a straight-side type (*left*) available. With straight-sided tyres the inside of the wheel itself was modified.

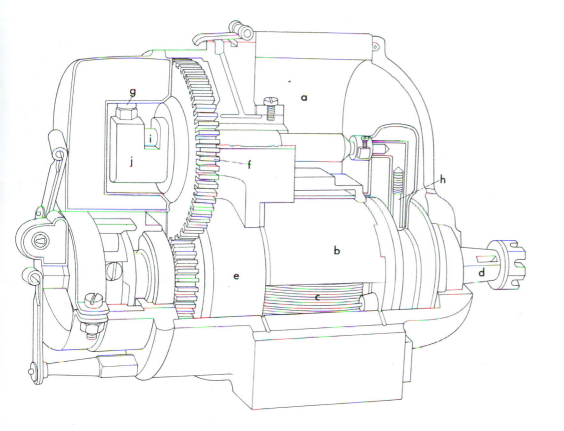

Sectioned view of a high-tension magneto, still the standard source of sparks in 1925, and common enough in 1931, when some twenty-five per cent of models on the British market still used it. It limited the functions of a battery to providing current for lights and ancillaries but was less well suited for quick morning starts, since it gave a weaker spark at low revs. It was also costlier to make (well, that is) than a coil, and those who fought on the Allied side in 1914 suffered seriously from the loss of Bosch, essentially a general provider in Europe. Logically, its future, such as it was, lay with super-sports and racing engines, and only ten per cent of all catalogued types had magnetos by 1935. (a) Magnet. (b) Armature core. (c) Windings. (d) Driving end. (e) Condenser. (f) Distributor gearwheel. (g) Carbon brush. (h) Pick-up brush. (i) Rotor. (j) Distributor.

Not that the spread of mass production transmitted Packard or Rolls-Royce quality to the middle-class sector of the market. What it did was to render the vehicle more acceptable practically to folk whose engineering knowledge was nil, and who could not afford "motor servants". Their prime requirement was to get from A to B more freely, more comfortably, and, if possible, more cheaply.

Hence, manufacturers of the 1920s administered pain-killers in place of the superb workmanship of the Golden Age. Engine speeds went up, giving the driver greater control of his machine. Power units were given full-pressure lubrication, which meant (in theory) only occasional toppings-up with oil, and the unintelligible magneto gave way to the simple battery and coil. By 1919, electric lighting had become a "must", even if the more dedicated cost-cutters clung to such crudities as Ford's magneto-driven headlamps (still available in 1925) and the acetylene illuminations found on French cyclecars, quite simply because full electrics would have landed the vehicles in a higher taxation class. In the same period, the electric starter progressed from being a high-cost option in Europe to a standard fixture, omitted at the maker's peril. Such a state of affairs had, in any case, obtained in the United States since 1915.

Starting-handles caused broken arms; inadequate anchors caused skids and fatalities. Hence, brakes received major attention during the decade. True, four-wheel brakes had been known in 1910, but an early preference for the uncoupled type (remember Austin Sevens in the 1920s!) had done nothing to increase their popularity. Thus, in 1919, France's Delages and Hispano-Suizas were virtually the only cars with a brake drum on each wheel, even if Duesenberg's advanced hydraulics lay only a year in the future. The speed with which the new idiom spread can best be assessed from the annual design summaries published in *The Autocar*. These, admittedly, covered only cars on the British market, but they are none the less illuminating. Four-wheel brakes received no mention in 1922, yet a year later, 28.5 per cent of all models had them as standard. The percentage rose to 47 in 1924, and 75 in 1925. In 1927, the last time a statistical breakdown was deemed necessary, only 6 per cent held out against progress, this despite the fact that only a short while back correspondents in the journal were inveighing against the idea as "an invitation to reckless high speed". But then Britain was rather a special case; she was bedevilled with a blanket speed limit of 20 mph (32 km/h) and would continue to be so beset until 1930.

Tyre life had also to be extended. Nineteen twenty-three saw the first wide-section, low-pressure "balloon" tyres, capable of absorbing the impact of a baulk of timber at 20 mph. "Balloons" were, in fact, claimed as the panacea for almost everything: better comfort on rough roads, less stress for the axles, longer tyre and chassis life, and freedom from skids thanks to superior road contact. Unfortunately, this new development coincided with front-wheel brakes, with results that were sometimes peculiar.

Early contracting-type front-wheel brakes were dirt-prone and not a great improvement on the two-wheel systems they replaced. Worse still, the manufacturers failed to recognize that the addition of anchors to front axles not designed to take the additional torque was an invitation to disaster. Add the extra weight of the new "balloons", and the result was the dreaded "shimmy", a disease worse than the side-slip of earlier days. It was not until 1927 that revised axle and steering layouts had eliminated the teething troubles of the new combination.

Next to receive attention was bodywork. In those days of composite wood-and-metal construction, open tourers were cheaper to make; they were also a great deal lighter. They were not, however, truly all-weather bodies, for all the elaborate arrangement of side-curtains affected by

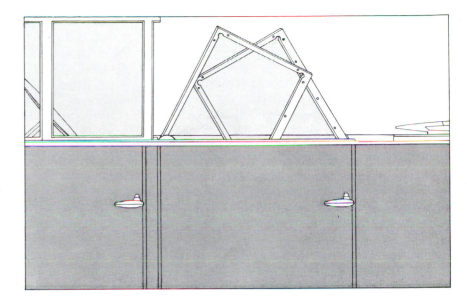

Damn-the-cost luxury at its best, 1930. Rolls-Royce's Phantom II (*left*) was launched at the 1929 Shows, and was conservative in that its makers clung to six cylinders at a time when Isotta Fraschini had been making straight-eights for a decade, and so had Duesenberg. Output from the 7.7-litre overhead-valve motor was "sufficient" (in fact, about 120 hp in 1930), and with reasonable bodywork, 90 mph (145 km/h) were possible. The car stopped superbly, thanks to the Hispano-type servo brakes. As even the short chassis measured 144 in (3.6 m) between wheel centres, there was plenty of room for the ultimate in coachwork, such as this sporting sedanca de ville (Americans would call it a town car) with the semi-cycle fenders, step plates instead of running boards, and the sidemounted spare wheels then fashionable. Cost? Anything from £2,900 to £3,300 ($14,500–$16,500), at a time when a working man with a job could expect to bring home £3 ($15) a week.

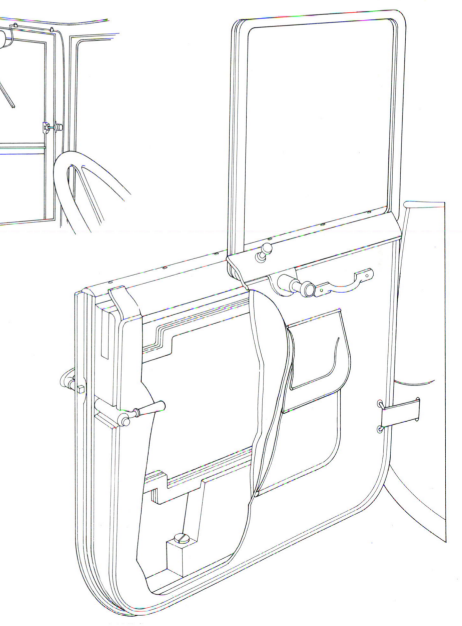

Weather protection to sedan standards on a touring car. Three specimens of Humber technique from the mid-twenties. Though celluloid was still used for side-curtains (*top right*), it was compressed into rigid frames to avoid distortion. Better still, the curtains retracted into the window and body framing, thus eliminating awkward storage problems (on other cars, they occupied the door pockets). The Humber windshield (*centre*) was a cumbersome four-panel affair, but this at least offered a degree of controlled ventilation. On a relatively expensive car, a windshield wiper (on the driver's side only, of course), was already standard equipment, while the strong clasps between the panels were said to be rattle-proof. (*Bottom right*) The neat way in which side-curtains were stowed. The curtains were split in half, a leather tab was used to raise and lower them, and once the two sections were up, they were secured by clasps similar to those on the windshield. In the lowered position, the curtains were insulated by felt pads which cut out further rattles.

such makers as Humber in Britain, which, like the American "California" tops, added weight and defeated the whole object. Lancia's detachable top, to be replaced by a canvas affair in summer, presented storage problems.

Little better were the early "all-weather" (five-passenger convertible sedan) styles affected by Britons and Frenchmen alike. These styles resulted in even heavier weights, and the top was a two-man affair, whatever catalogues claimed. Thus, only a sizable price differential could keep the tourer in its position of pre-eminence.

There were, of course, closed bodies available on inexpensive chassis. Most American makers were offering permanent-top sedans by 1918 – at a price. Even in 1921, the differential could be as much as eighty per cent: compare the $1,695 asked for a Maxwell sedan with the $995 asked for the tourer. The Ford at $760 was cheap enough, but it could not compete with open cars at $415. A Buick Six with a $1,795 price-tag was elevated into the luxury class if winter comforts were required.

In 1922, Hudson's breakthrough on the Essex Four, with a mere $300 differential between open and closed models, paved the way to a new era. By 1927, only $5 separated a tourer from the cheapest five-passenger sedan.

With Europe's smaller volume sales, of course, such minimal differentials were not viable, though the same trend was reflected in the fact that the prices of open and closed Morris-Cowleys fell by twenty-six per cent between 1925 and 1931. Purchasers of the more expensive Oxford fared rather better; only four per cent was slashed off tourers, but

thanks to the new Pressed Steel plant, sedans became twenty-five per cent cheaper.

Low prices generate demand, and further demand forces them still lower. By 1928, eighty-five per cent of all new cars sold in the United States carried closed bodywork, and some interesting price patterns were emerging. While Ford and Chevrolet still sold enough roadsters and tourers to list these as bargain-basement items, the cheapest Buicks, Essexes, Graham-Paiges, Hudsons, and Oldsmobiles – to name but a few breeds – were coaches (two-door sedans). In some cases, the open-car package was jazzed up with wire wheels and dual side-mounted spares to justify the extra manufacturing cost of what was fast becoming a special-order item, retained in the catalogue to keep faith with the customers. Hupmobile charged a $145 premium for a roadster and a whopping $175 for a phaeton; even the four-door sedans were cheaper.

Thus, the open models were slowly phased out. Buick, who had sold nearly 41,000 phaetons in 1925, broke 10,000 of this style for the last time in 1927, while only 4,650 of the 53,000 Chryslers made in 1931 carried open bodies. Ford disposed of over 200,000 Model A roadsters in 1929, but even the Depression cannot alone account for the total of 15,000 roadsters and phaetons sold in 1932. Henceforward, the celluloid side-curtain would be virtually confined to sporting machinery. Attempts to revive it on both sides of the Atlantic after the Second World War – Dodge's Wayfarer and the Morris Minor – met with a cool reception, both cars soon acquiring proper wind-up windows.

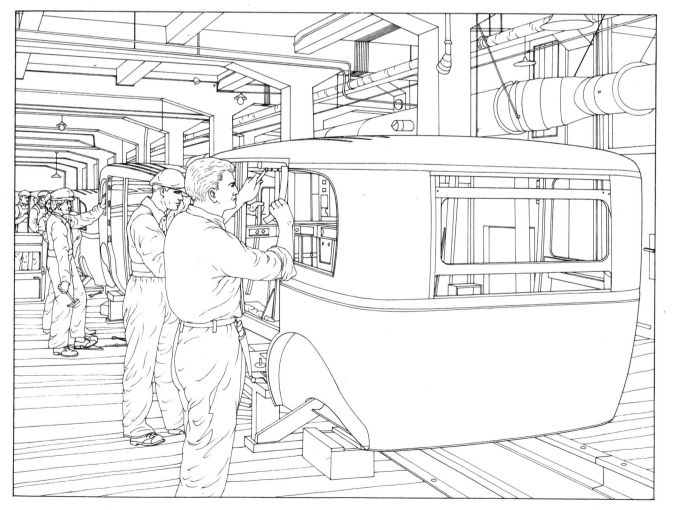

(*Left*) Handwork is much in evidence on the Volvo body line in 1929. The composite construction is obvious: it was a case of fitting together a series of fairly small panels, since Volvo, still a modest outfit, had no large presses. If the tempo of this factory scene seems leisurely, one must remember that Volvo's total production of sixes that year was precisely 386 units.

(*Opposite, top*) Anatomy of a family automobile at the beginning of our period. In fact, Volvo's PV652 was fairly advanced for its time, with its hydraulic brakes, the one feature which stamps it as essentially early thirties rather than vintage. For the rest, there is little one would not have encountered any time from about 1923 onwards–a simple channel-section frame with four cross-members, a semi-elliptic leaf spring at each corner, and a front-mounted engine driving the rear wheels. Unit gearboxes had, of course, long been majority practice (and pretty well universal on mass-produced cars) but engines still sat well back behind the front axle centre-line, and thus space was wasted.

(*Opposite, bottom*) Making a car, 1929. This drawing from Volvo shows the assembly of chassis and body, and their ultimate marriage. In those pre-unitary days, the two elements had to do a fair amount of travelling before they came together. Not that new methods necessarily put a stop to this: in unitary times, the press-work specialists were often responsible for the entire chassis-body structure, which was then transported to the official "factory" to receive its engine, transmission, axles, and running gear. Interesting is the adoption of a moving assembly line in a small venture.

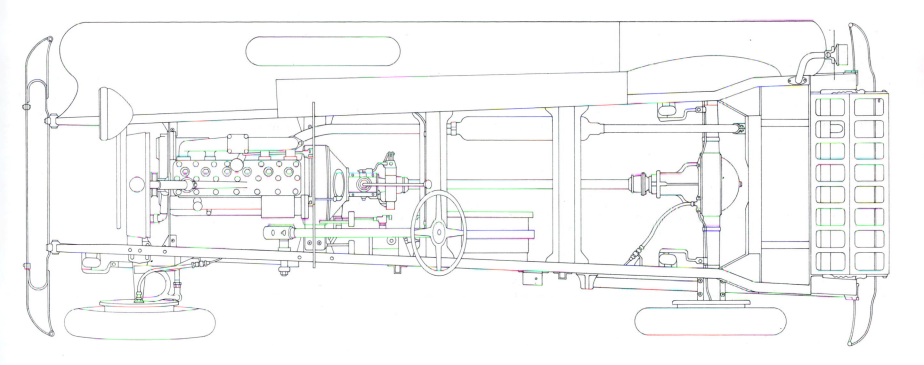

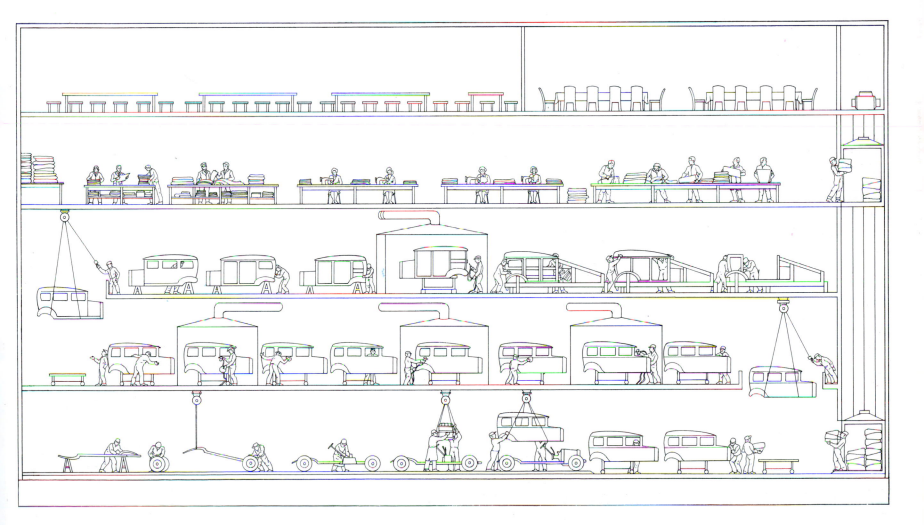

Terribly, terribly British, or what the Anglo-Saxons do best. (*Left*) The 1930 M-type MG Midget. The body was fabric covered, flimsy (it only cost its makers £6.50 or $32.50), and claustrophobic with the top up, actual output from the 847-cc overhead-camshaft engine was a mere 20 hp, and the two-bearing crankshaft wasn't exactly adamantine. However, 60–65 mph (100–110 km/h) were yours for a mere £185 ($925), and as the basis was Morris Minor, there were parts and service in every English town. The office (*bottom*) is a little cramped, and the vee windshield doesn't really help. This example has black-face dials of obvious Morris origin: later ones had white faces. The gearshift is awkward: a quick change from low to second can impale one's hand against the facia, a good reason why later clients often chose the fourspeed option with MG's famous remote lever.

The MG sold. The 21-hp Speed Model Sunbeam four-door coupé (*opposite*) didn't, largely because its main competitor was Talbot of London, a member of the same group and more dynamic in design and marketing. Neither firm considered rationalization, so by 1935, when this car was made, the receivers were in. The Sunbeam combined elegance, handling, and a comfortable cruising speed of 70 mph (112 km/h). The trouble was that not many people had £800 ($4,000) to burn, and there was plenty of choice in this sector – Alvis and Lagonda as well as Talbot.

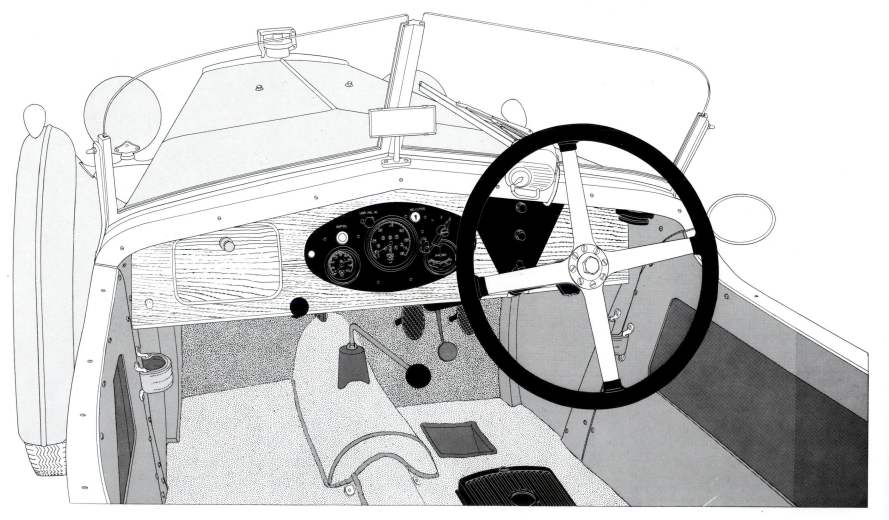

The Model A, Ford's second "Universal Car", shown (*top left*) in original 1928 roadster form and (*top right*) as a 1930 Fordor sedan. The difference between the two is essentially stylistic, though the observant will note that, on the drawing (*below*) showing one of the first chassis, the handbrake (*a*) is on the driver's side, whereas early in 1928, it was moved to the centre. The car was very much Every-man's Transport, its reliable, slow-turning, 3.3-litre four-cylinder engine giving 40 hp and propelling it at 60–65 mph (100–105 km/h). The delightfully simple three-speed transmission (*b*) marked a major departure from the T's pedal-controlled shift, but at long last, it enabled anyone who could drive a Ford to handle anything else and would eventu-ally eliminate those special "planetary" drivers' licences issued by certain states to those whose experience did not extend beyond Lizzie. Most of the engineering was now copybook American: thermo-syphon cooling (*c*), coil ignition (*d*), hydrau-lic dampers (*e*), and a spiral bevel back axle (*f*). Ford, like Chevrolet, favoured torque tube drive (*g*), and it was still accepted practice to mount ignition and throttle controls (*h*) on the steering wheel. The wheel itself (*i*) had a diameter of 18 in (45.5 cm) – bus-size by the standards of our times. Primitive influences, of course, remained: Henry Ford was obstinately loyal to his transverse-leaf suspension (*j*) at both ends, giving excellent performance over farm tracks and bouncy rides on the highway. He also distrusted fuel pumps, retaining gravity feed from a dash tank (*k*). The mechanical four-wheel

brakes (*l*) were adequate only for a car of such modest performance. The Model A was manufactured or assembled, to the tune of over five million units in many countries, and as late as the mid-sixties over three hundred thousand were said still to be in daily use in the United States. What is also soon forgotten is that the model formed the entire basis for the Soviet automotive industry, going into production as the GAZ-A at Gorki in 1931. In the pre-Second World War period, it was virtually Russia's staple au-tomobile, and truck editions (GAZ-AA) were still being made in 1948.

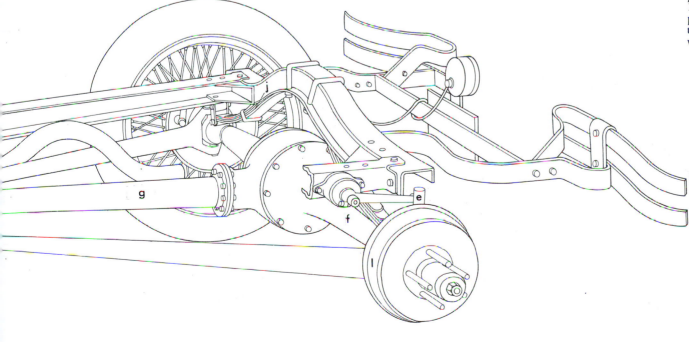

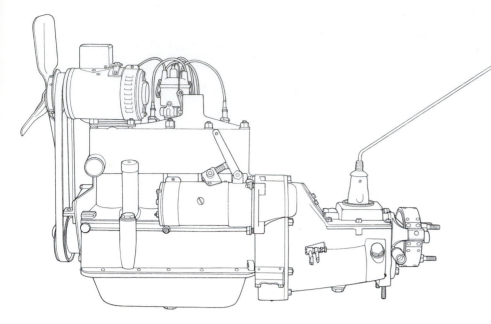

Resembling a 1930–31 American car in miniature, the original 1932 Fiat 508 Balilla was very European indeed beneath the surface. Dimensions were compact, with a wheel-base of 88.5 in (2.25 m) and an overall length of only 136 in (3.45 m). The 995-cc engine (*top left*) was modern to the extent of having nearly "square" dimensions (65×75 mm), but it was still a straightforward side-valve giving 22 hp. Coil ignition is to be expected, but a virtue not found on some later overhead-valve Fiats was the high mounting of generator and distributor, rendering the unit almost impervious to floods. The three-speed transmission is mounted in unit with the single-plate clutch, there would be no synchromesh before 1934, and a curious survival (easily seen in the engine picture, though less so in the sectioned view) was

the "sudden-death" transmission brake – immensely effective, but strictly for parking, unless one fancied buying a pair of new axle shafts. The transitional nature of the engineering is more clearly detectable in the cutaway view. Advanced on a small and cheap car are the cruciform-braced frame (*a*) and hydraulic brakes (*b*), neither of them features to be found on 1932's other babies. Shock absorbers (*c*) are also hydraulic, while nobody would expect independent suspension as early as this, except maybe in Germany. The long and willowy gearshift lever (*d*) reflects contemporary American influence. Coming to details, a single overslung windshield wiper (*e*) was all one got in the under-£200 (say $1,000) class, while wire wheels and bumpers were also on the extras list. Perhaps the most obvious hallmarks of an earlier age are up-draught carburation (*f*) and the fuel tank on the firewall (*g*). This latter was foolproof provided feed pipes did not clog, but it was hardly very safe. Not visible here are the hand throttle (still general practice but retained on Fiats long after it disappeared from other makes) and the curious plunger type ignition key (one rotated it to operate the lights). Curious things happened when the switch-wards began to wear, and it was not proof against the attentions of ignorant car-park attendants! Launched in the depth of the Depression, the original three-speed Balilla sold over forty-one thousand units in two years, and the later four-speeders did even better, the side-valve line continuing until mid-1937. The model was built under licence in Czechoslovakia, Poland, Germany, and France. The French Balilla, rated at 6CV, became the world-famous Simca.

Also doomed were finishes which required more than a quick wipe-over. The new generation of motorists might not do their own maintenance – indeed, they were discouraged from so doing. Ford had long since instituted flat-rating practices throughout their dealer network, and the other American and European mass-producers would soon follow suit. The new motorists did, however, like something that was easy to clean – the Instant Car Wash did not exist, even in the United States – not to mention a coat of paint likely to outlive their own spell of ownership. DuPont's Duco cellulose had first been seen on the 1924 Oaklands, and by 1928, it was general practice outside the realm of the specialist coachbuilder, who would adopt it in the early 1930s. Hot on its heels came non-tarnishable chromium-plated brightwork. Considered vulgar and meretricious by many – Gabriel Voisin said he would adopt it "when Cartier sells artificial pearls" – it had crossed the Atlantic by 1929 and was probably the most important cosmetic change of the 1930 season.

All these were American innovations. One component, however, survived the 1920s without major change, and that was the gearbox.

Its concomitants, admittedly, did not. The cone clutch, fairly general practice in 1920 and still common in 1925, had been ousted by the single dry-plate type, though Morris and Hudson would keep their smooth wet-plate units right up to the end of the 1930s. "Fierce" has long been the accepted epithet for the old cones, and some of them were just that.

The type's one unpardonable sin was, however, that it required regular maintenance if it were to keep its good manners, and the new generation wanted no truck with dressings, let alone propping the pedal out overnight.

There had also been a change in shift levers, from the old visible gate to the simpler and less pleasing ball type, while more and more cars kept their "change-speed levers" in the centre.

Nobody will ever agree which came first – left-hand steering or centre shift – but both were logical in a country such as the United States, which had a right-hand rule-of-the-road; by 1916, a virtual uniformity prevailed throughout the American industry. Though Packard tried briefly to maintain the traditional image with a left-hand gear-shift as well, centrally-mounted levers (which meant the hand-brake, too) permitted entry and exit from either side, and therefore four doors on four-passenger car bodies. Early European converts to centre shift were Citroën (who made both left-hand and right-hand drive cars) and Morris (who would not bother with left hook until 1934), but Continental makers generally were slow to adopt the "American" driving position. In France and Germany, however, left-hand drive was in the majority by 1925, though in Italy only Fiat would take it up, from 1927 onwards. Upper-class makers, especially the French and Italian ones, preferred right-hand steering because it made sense on Alpine passes; the French *grandes routières* wore it obstinately to the bitter end, and left-hook Lancias were the direct result of an attack on the American market in 1956. In Britain, of course, right-hand floor shift had a long innings in front of it; the arrangement was *de rigueur* on upper-class machinery in 1930 (Sunbeam, for instance, supplied a central lever only to special order), while Rolls-Royce and Bentley fitted it to the final days of manual-transmission cars some twenty-seven years later.

In other respects, this conservative approach to transmissions may seem curious. What Americans disliked, they tended to jettison, this going for the transmission brake, almost extinct in the United States at this stage, and restricted to an emergency role elsewhere since the advent of front-wheel brakes. They disliked shifting gears even more; so why, then, did synchromesh not make its appearance until 1929 (on Cadillacs and La Salles), while Europe's preselectors, already listed on

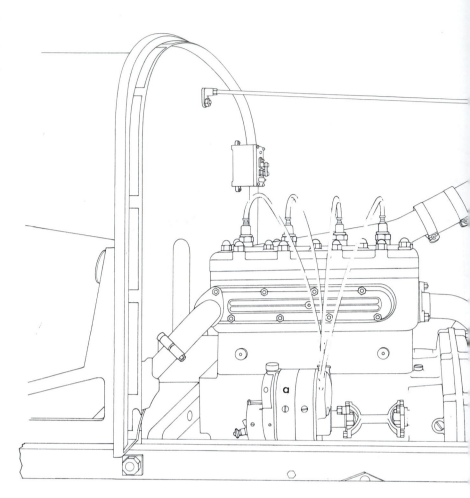

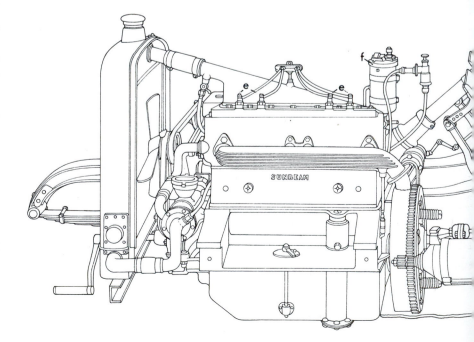

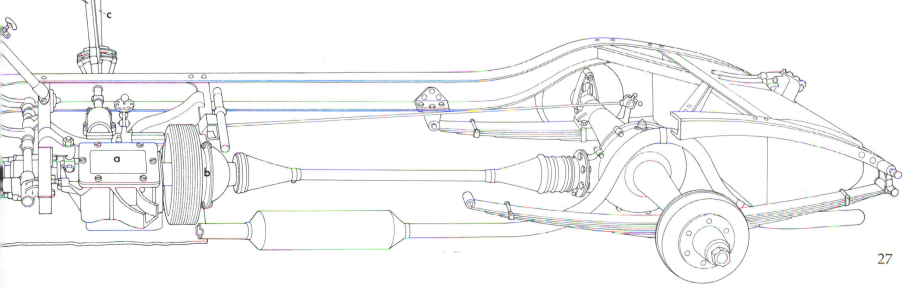

(*Top left*) It looks old, and it is – the engine of the first-ever Citroën, 1919's A type four of 1,327 cc. But there isn't a lot that couldn't have been there in 1930. Of the three elements which date this unit, only one, the magneto (*a*) was still common on tourers of a decade later. A closer look will reveal the exposed tubes (*b*) of the radiator (these would not have been visible even from the front in the thirties) and the high-pressure tyre (*c*) on beaded-edge rims.

(*Below*) When the post-war Sunbeam was announced in 1919, much was made of its "complete electrical equipment". Well it

might, for the 3-litre four-cylinder Sixteen had been around since 1911! Nevertheless, the cylinders are cast monobloc, and you can't always spot high stroke-bore ratios (the Sunbeam's was 1.9:1) from the apparent depth of the block. The more obvious dating features are the separate gearbox (*a*) with the transmission brake (*b*) behind. The right-hand gearshift (*c*) works in a visible gate, and beside it is a man-sized lever (*d*) for the "service" brake. Compression taps (*e*) for priming the cylinders were something that went out with the advent of manually-operated chokes, though the vacuum feed (*f*) from a rear tank was common throughout the

twenties and survived into the early thirties.

(*Top right*) Never be misled by the boxy looks of American cars of the mid-twenties, by the uncomfortable rumble seats of coupés like this 1927 Chrysler, or by that built-in nuisance, the fixed wood wheel, with its demountable rim. Beneath the skin, the Model-70, as it was known, was one of the best all-round big-car buys of that year. The designation spelt out the maximum speed in mph, which required no special tuning to attain; 68 hp from 3.6 litres was excellent going for those days.

27

Looking Ahead. The BMW Type 315/1 of 1934 is, of course, eclipsed by the legendary 328, surely the best all-rounder of the 1930s. People also tend to be unkind about the 315's ancestry: it was descended from the German Austin Seven via the 303, a pint-sized 1.2-litre six that performed little better than its British contemporaries. The 303 had a short life, but it left some useful legacies – a light twin-tube frame, transverse-leaf independent front suspension, a four-bearing pushrod engine, and a four-speed synchromesh transmission. The stock 315 with single carburettor and 34 hp was fairly uninspired, but the sports model's extra carburettor helped boost output of the 1,490-cc unit to 40 hp and speed to the middle 70s (120 km/h). The cars sold well in Central Europe and Scandinavia, as well as in Britain, where Frazer Nash took them up and were soon doing better with modern Germans than ever they had with their own strictly-bespoke chain-driven machinery. The BMW's brakes were mechanical (though hydraulics had been used on the 303), but by mid-1935, there was a companion 2-litre on the same chassis, sports versions of which were good for over 80 mph (130–135 km/h) on 55 hp. Sales in four seasons amounted to 9,765 315s and 6,646 of the bigger 319s, a creditable performance for the period.

the largest Armstrong Siddeleys, would never make any lasting impact at all?

The plain fact was that Americans chose to dispense with shifting altogether by devoting their efforts to big, slow-turning multi-cylinder engines that did all their work in high gear. Only the steepest hill or worst traffic snarls called for an indirect ratio: "0–70, and never a hand on the lever", was one of the safest and most persistent publicity themes. There was no substitute for cubic inches – or for more cylinders.

The first commercially viable six-cylinder car, of course, dates back to 1904, and the configuration had enjoyed a substantial vogue between 1906 and 1908, with some support from the young proprietary-engine industry. This craze was, however, short-lived; a brief world depression did not help, two extra "pots" meant two more of everything else, and Frederick Lanchester had yet to solve the problems of crankshaft balance. Long and whippy shafts led to tooth-shaking vibration periods. In 1907, Henry Ford might claim that he was the world's largest maker of six-cylinder automobiles, but within a couple of years, he (and almost everyone else) was back with fours. It was thus left to his compatriots to reinstate the type, which they had done by the outbreak of the First World War. By 1918, Cadillac's vee-eight and Packard's vee-twelve were established successes, even if in Europe multi-cylinderism was still the prerogative of the town carriage.

Multi-cylinderism spread down the American market from middle-class to cheap automobiles. In 1924, the four best-selling makes – Ford, Chevrolet, Dodge, and Willys-Overland – offered fours and fours alone, but five years later, Dodge and Chevrolet had added an extra pair of cylinders, John N. Willys backed his successful Whippet Four with a 3-litre six, and the only new four of any significance was Chrysler's Plymouth, a direct descendant of the once-popular Maxwell. And for those who considered a six inadequate, there was the straight-

eight, not only smoother than the familiar vees, but blending well with a new stylistic idiom that called for lengthy hoods. The ultimate in multi-cylinderism would arrive, as we shall see, at the depth of the Depression, though it was undoubtedly conceived during the euphoric wave that preceded the stock market crash.

Smaller sixes were also on the way in Europe. In 1925, Renault's most modest six had run to 4.8 litres, while the comparable 510 Fiat was a 3.4-litre town carriage best suited to a paid driver. Opel were likewise toying with some hefty and expensive machinery, but only one British volume-producer (Singer) had a six-cylinder car on the market, and they sold precious few of these. At a higher level, Crossley of Manchester were boasting that four of their cylinders were as good as six of anyone else's, which did not, however, stop them launching their 2.7-litre 18/50 a year later – or selling it to members of the British Royal Family! The 1927 shows, however, would see an interesting race of scaled-down Americana. From Britain came Rover's 2-litre, the 2.2-litre Austin Sixteen, and the 2.5 litre JA-series Morris; Fiat countered with the Tipo 520; and Renault (already doing well with the 3.2-litre Vivasix announced a year previously) were exploring the ultimate in flexibility and gutlessness with the 1.4-litre Mona series. The pint-sized six, however, belongs properly to the 1930s; suffice it to say for the moment that, of the principal cheap European sedans in the 1,900- to 2,500-cc bracket listed in 1930, only such stalwarts as the Austin 12 and the KZ-type Renault remained faithful to four cylinders, and both these were listed alongside parallel sixes. Hillman's 14 had an even less felicitous stablemate in the shape of an unreliable straight-eight, while even the smaller national producers – Skoda of Czechoslovakia and Volvo of Sweden – fell into line. Further, though the Depression would decimate the ranks of the eights – of which there were some ten at peak in Germany alone – most of the sixes would see the lean years out.

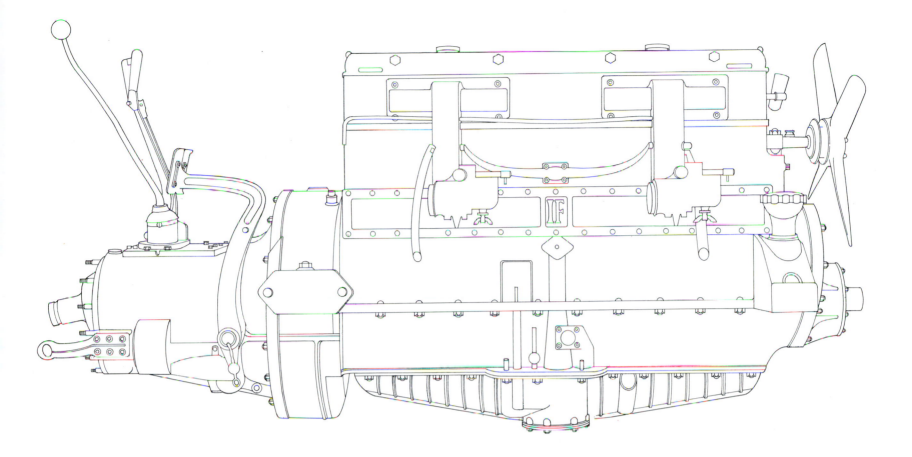

How many cylinders? For luxury and for cars to be driven in, the straight-eight was undoubtedly the smoothest unit in general use in the 1920s, and Isotta Fraschini (*top*) had made nothing else since 1919. This was one of their last, the 8B of 1931–34, with twin Zenith carburettors and an output of 160 hp from 7.4 litres. By the 1930s, a unit gearbox was no longer a heresy in the luxury class, though outside the United States few other makers still considered three speeds sufficient. Certainly they weren't on the 4½-litre Bentley (*below*), where the four forward ratios were high and close and selected on many open models by a right-hand lever mounted *outside* the body. The sixteen-valved overhead-camshaft engine ran to only four cylinders, and ignition was by dual magneto. The standard article, still being made in 1931, gave 110 hp and speeds of 90–95 mph (145–155 km/h), but with the optional supercharger, the main limitation was wind resistance, of which the Bentley had enough! The car was an anachronism, but a splendid one. No wonder some conservative clients preferred the four, with its "bloody thump", signally absent from the companion 6½-litre six.

(*Left*) Volvo in 1933, or a conventional shape covering conventional engineering. The "sit" of the wheels confirms beam axles at both ends, and nothing is streamlined in, least of all the spare wheels in those deep wells: hard work for the girls in the event of a flat, and lovely rain-water traps. The roof-line is more curved than it was in 1929, and the three-speed transmission incorporates a free wheel as well as synchromesh. This device rendered shifting entirely clutchless and improved fuel economy at the price of a loss of engine braking, which is why the more enthusiastic motorist tended to lock the device out and ignore it. As always, your Volvo Six came in a diversity of forms. Standard sedans like this one came on a 116-in (2.95 m) wheel-base, but there were two longer variants for the taxi trade, and an ultra-elongated type for "parade cabriolets", ambulances, and hearses. Such diversification was not peculiar to Volvo; Packard and Cadillac rang the changes on chassis length as well.

(*Below*) The price of an impressive hood and the purr of eight cylinders in line was wasted space, only too clear in this shot of a 1931 first-series CD-type Chrysler unit of 4 litres' capacity. The power unit is classically American – there's just more of it. The down-draught carburettor is not clearly visible, but its air cleaner is. The transmission is, of course, in unit with clutch and engine, but the shift lever has to "come easily to hand", and so it is long,

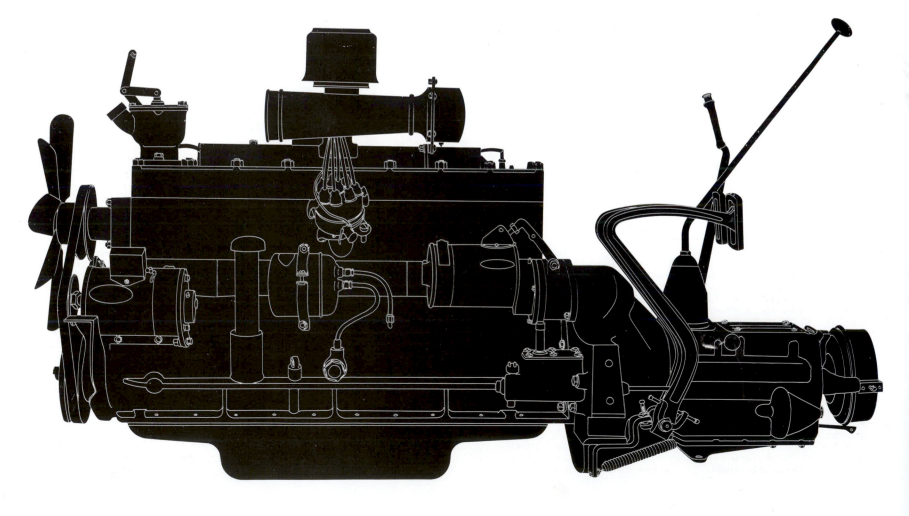

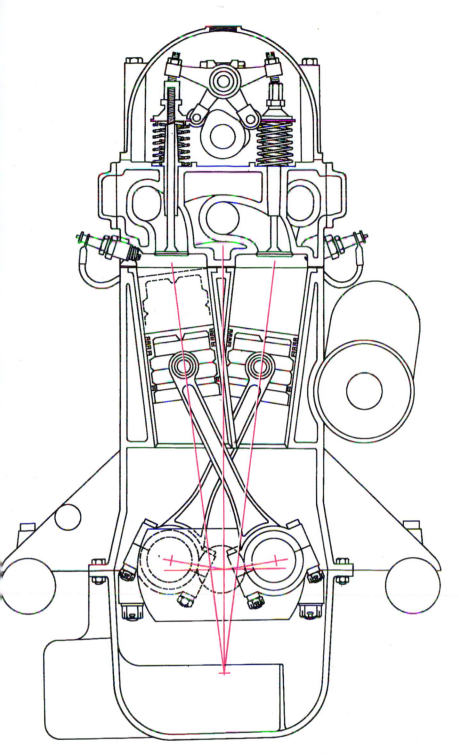

With mass-production came some interesting strides in overall performance. Contrast, for instance, that pioneer of the system, Citroën's 1919 Model A, with its 1929 successor, the AC4.

Engine capacity has gone up by twenty-three per cent – from 1,327 to 1,628 cc – and the 1929 engine is still a side-valve monobloc four. The increase in output – from 18 to 30 bhp – represents, however, a formidable sixty-six per cent, and the AC4 develops its maximum power at 3,000 rpm, not 2,000. Further, while three forward speeds still suffice, the new Citroën rides on a more robust frame with semi-elliptic instead of quarter-elliptic springs, and balloon tyres at 25–30 psi give a softer ride than the old beaded-edge type running at a pressure of 60 psi. There is a lot more car for the money, too: the A-type on its wheelbase of 111.5 in (2.835 m) was a cramped four-seater with only a single door, whereas the AC4 comes as a fully-enclosed, all-steel four-door sedan. Yet it occupies little more space; half an inch of wheelbase and four inches of overall length. The extra weight – 800 lbs (360 kg) odd – has been fully absorbed by the more powerful engine, as is discovered when one takes the wheel. The A-type was flat out at 40 mph (65 km/h), cruising gait being a leisured 37 mph; the 1929 car is good for 56 mph (90 km/h) and settles down comfortably at 47 mph (75 km/h). Fuel consumption, admittedly, is higher, but then fuel is cheaper, and the AC4 with its coil ignition is easier to service. With servo-assisted four-wheel brakes replacing the old rear-wheel and transmission layout, the car stops better. No detailed figures are available for the two Citroëns, but they are available for a brace of comparable Fiats, the 1919 501 and the 1,438-cc 514 introduced late in 1929. The former took a daunting 183 ft (86 m) to pull up from its normal cruising speed of 40 mph, but the latter managed it in 80 ft (24 m), a good year before the colossus of Turin switched to hydraulic actuation. Useless to observe, as vintage-minded diehards will, that the 501 had an engine of sewing-machine sweetness and a delicacy of control which the 514 signally lacked. The latter had all the modern conveniences; it also cost a lot less, being made in relatively larger numbers. Despite the Depression, 514s left the works at a rate of twelve thousand units a year as against eleven thousand for the earlier type. A more significant comment is that the new idiom called for more frequent model changes; the 501, launched at the time of the 1918 Armistice, was still around seven years later, whereas the 514 survived for precisely three model-years—from 1930 to 1932 inclusive.

This highlights one of the less happy aspects of the mass-production game. It could resemble a football league contest run on knockout rules. The choice lies between taking on the big battalions or facing relegation; there is no third division to assure at least a degree of survival for the failures. By 1930, the industry had crystallized into four main sectors: the big volume producers catering for the masses, the middle-class makers bidding in a higher price bracket, the manufacturers of luxury vehicles, and the specialists. A big combine of the type already operative in the United States needed to compete in at least three of these four categories. The same went for their European opposite numbers – in the 1930s, Nuffield in Britain and Auto Union in Germany. This latter empire sold DKWs to the masses, Wanderers to the middle class, and Horchs to the wealthy, success in these three fields compensating for the failure of the front-wheel drive Audi in the specialist sector. Since the latter's sole asset was elegance, one need not wonder that the division reverted to conventional drive on its 1939 models.

The specialists need not concern us at this stage. Their survival depends only on the whims of a tiny minority of the motoring public – and, therefore, on their ability to change direction at the right moment. Morgan's switch from three to four wheels in 1936 typifies such a timely

willowy, and not much more positive in action than the horrible column changes of 1938 onwards. Unusual on an American car is the drum-type transmission brake, strictly for parking. This device was never popular in the United States (when Fiat started to manufacture in New York State in the 'teens, they dropped it from their local variations), but Chrysler defended it on the grounds that it left the entire rear-wheel braking area free for the normal business of stopping!

(*Above*) *Multum in parvo* – or how to evolve a really compact engine without losing out on power. Your usual vee motor had a 60- or 90-degree angle, but during our period (and before), Lancia worked to angles which could be as narrow as 13 degrees and never exceeded 24. This is the original 1922 2.1-litre four-cylinder Lambda (still current in enlarged form as late as 1932), but the technique was applied to everything from the tiny 903-cc Ardea up to big vee-eights like the 4-litre Dilambda. Advantages were a short and rigid crankshaft, a square, box-shaped head with better water circulation, and a simpler valve gear – note the use of a single overhead camshaft where wider vees (the post-war Ferrari and Jaguar, for instance) required one per bank of cylinders. The Lambda block was only 15.5 in (39.4 cm) long, which meant not only more room for passengers, but also underhood access to transmission as well as engine.

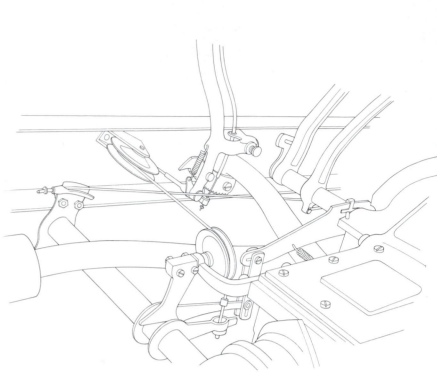

Looking at the 1930 Nash Eight (*above*) one wonders that it still used cable-operated brakes as seen in the drawing (*right*). Would not Americans have sought ways round the constant need of adjustment? The fact was that cables were trusted more than fluids and rubber piping. Of thirty American breeds with pretensions to volume production in 1930, only nine were addicted to hydraulics, these headed by the Chrysler Corporation stable (Chrysler, De Soto, Dodge, and Plymouth). Other significant supporters were Franklin and Graham-Paige: General Motors would not join in till 1934, nor Ford till 1939. The Nash Eight itself, though conventional enough in appearance, had two unusual features: overhead

salvation. Nor were the purveyors of true luxury doomed until after the Second World War – if Minerva and Isotta Fraschini failed to see the decade out, Rolls-Royce, Maybach, and Packard were still very much alive in 1939. But in the two lower echelons – from the Chevrolet–Citroën level to that of Buick and Humber – a savagely competitive element intrudes, with a knock-out battle of manufacturers spanning the inter-war years. The speed of such a battle is geared to the strength of an individual country's industry and of the market it serves, but the result is invariable – fewer manufacturers making more cars at more competitive prices. What started in the United States in 1923 would be reflected in the boom-ridden Japan of the mid-1960s.

In the United States, of course, the biggest combine – and in effect the only one in 1919 – was General Motors, which covered everything from the cut-price Chevrolet up to the Cadillac, by no means the leading luxury marque in those days. Ford had no volume-selling companion car until Lincoln added their cheap V12 Zephyr in 1936, while Walter Chrysler's big build-up occurred in 1928, when he absorbed the profitable Dodge concern and created two brand-new makes, the inexpensive Plymouth and the intermediate De Soto. Yet, in 1928, the Big Three commanded a sizable percentage of the national take – nearly fifty-five per cent of the 4.5 million new automobiles delivered that year.

Thus, a squeeze was inevitable. First to go were the smaller assemblers, whose function was often little more than adding a radiator with badge to an assortment of bought-out components. Typical of these was the Anderson Motor Company, based at Rock Hill, South Carolina, remote from the mainstream industry, despite the fact that it produced something more than a regional make. Advertising was organized on a national basis, and the annual sales potential was, perhaps, three thousand units, all in the capricious middle-class market. Such a set-up

was just viable in 1920, but hopeless in the accelerating tempo of ensuing years. The Anderson Motor Company had called it quits by 1926. Assembled breeds with some cachet – the Jordan, for instance, with its brilliant publicity campaigns – just made it into 1931.

Next on the list of victims were manufacturers proper in the twelve to twenty thousand-a-year bracket, which was not enough to cover more than two sectors of the market. These companies were only safe as long as they retained their key middle-class clientele. In this category fell Chandler-Cleveland, Paige, and Reo; Hupmobile, with a potential of perhaps forty thousand, were higher up the scale but still vulnerable. Alas! middle-class sales were the most capricious and suffered worst in the Depression years. The companies took longer to die, but it was all over by Pearl Harbor. Chandler sold out to Hupmobile in 1929, and seven years later, Reo switched to trucks for good. Paige won a new lease of life in 1927, with the advent of the dynamic Graham brothers, but the resultant Graham-Paige Corporation was in for a slow decline from their 1929 peak of seventy-seven thousand cars. They tried hard with new ideas: the "twin-top" four-speed gearbox in 1929, the revolutionary Blue Streak styling of 1932, and the centrifugally-blown straight-eights of 1934. In 1935, they offered a cheap six at near-Chevrolet price, but even a merger with the ailing Hupmobile empire could not save them. The 1941 Grahams were the last.

Even empires could fall. William C. Durant made his last bid in 1921, with a line-up that embraced (at peak) a challenger for Ford and Chevrolet in the Star, the Durant which "marked" Oakland and Oldsmobile, the Flint in opposition to Buick and the new Chrysler, and the luxurious and conservative Locomobile, more exclusive than any Cadillac or Lincoln. Within two years, the new group had worked its sales up to 172,000 units, but this still gave them only fifth place, and it was a flash in the pan. In 1925, the introduction of an inexpensive

valves and dual ignition. Flathead motors were reserved for their cheaper lines. The big valve-in-head six (if not the eight, which faded in 1942) would continue to power the top Nashes until they started on short-stroke vee-eights in 1955. Many Europeans would regard this Lincoln as the archetype of the American car in the early thirties, and its elegant lines and lengthy hood are typical. The rest isn't, even if one almost expects to see Herbert Hoover or Franklin Delano Roosevelt waving from the back seat – Lincolns were favourite White House wear in those days. The huge K-series was current in various forms from 1932 to 1940, but seldom seen. In 1933, nearly 475,000 Americans bought new Chevrolets and another 335,000 new Fords, but Lincoln's total production was only just over 2,000 cars, and in those sedan-oriented days precisely 88 were tourings of any kind. The open car with side curtains was nearly as dead as the dodo. The few lucky owners, however, were well supplied for their money, usually around $4,500 (£900) of it. The precision built vee-twelve motor gave 150 hp from 7.2 litres, enough to assure this 5,250-pounder (say 2,375 kg) a top speed in the middle 90s (150 km/h).

straight-eight Locomobile gave even better market coverage, but thereafter, the path lay downhill. Nineteen twenty-seven was the Flint's last year, the Star died in 1928, and even token production of Locomobiles had ceased a twelvemonth later. By 1930, Durant's sole passenger-car offering was a six with prices starting at $645 (£120) – just too far above Chevrolet, and sales of 20,900 against Ford's 1,155,162 told their own story. Durant struggled into 1931 with a companion four, but that was the end. Subsequent American and Canadian attempts at a revival came to naught.

Even greater was the fall of Willys-Overland, in the big league since 1910 and never out of the top ten thereafter, despite a financial crisis in 1921. Willys sold 315,000 units in 1929, when their market coverage almost rivalled that of General Motors's, with prices running from $525 to $5,800 (£105 to £1,160). The company had assembly plants in Belgium and Britain, and even a German subsidiary, but the Depression, coupled with a sudden abdication from four-cylinder models, brought the empire down. True, it survived a protracted receivership, but though passenger-car manufacture was not finally abandoned until 1955, Willys would always be an also-ran.

The moral was simple: relegation point was rising inexorably from the three thousand units a year of the early 1920s. By 1931, Hupmobile could still just about make ends meet on annual deliveries of seventeen thousand, but when the "little recession" struck in 1938, sales of thirty-five thousand a year represented desperation point. Of that season's tail-enders, Pierce-Arrow were already bankrupt; Willys, Hupmobile, and Graham were destined for the axe; and Cadillac and De Soto were rescued only by their membership of the Big Battalions, who seldom risked scrapping a major line. (The sole exceptions in our period were two General Motors breeds, Oakland and La Salle. The former was quietly overwhelmed by its cheaper companion-make, Pontiac, while the La Salle was squeezed out by the bottom end of the Cadillac range and the more expensive Buicks). Nash alone rode out plummeting sales – and survived as an independent for another sixteen years. One may doubt if they would have achieved this but for the Second World War and the ensuing sellers' market.

This pattern of contraction would soon be reflected in Europe. Here small companies proliferated – and they went down like ninepins. In France conservatism and worn-out factories took their toll. So did pressure from the Big Three – Peugeot, Renault, and the upstart André Citroën. Clément-Bayard, Gobron-Brillié, and Mors barely survived the Armistice. The late 1920s would see the demise of such respected names as Charron, de Dion-Bouton, Hurtu, La Buire, Rolland-Pilain, and Turcat-Méry, while Léon Bollée and Rochet-Schneider quit in the early thirties. In Italy Itala never recovered from wartime mismanagement, though as late as 1934, attempts were made to keep things going. German casualties included Dürkopp, Loreley, Phänomen, Presto, and Protos, with NAG. following them into oblivion in 1934. The British story was much the same – as always, it was the middle-class producers who succumbed: Belsize in 1925, Arrol-Johnston in 1929, Star in 1931, in which year Lea-Francis suffered the first of several eclipses. Humber, Sunbeam, and Talbot were absorbed into the Rootes empire, Morris absorbed Wolseley, and Vauxhall became a subsidiary of General Motors, turning out cut-price cars and trucks. Lanchester, once the country's most individual luxury automobile, fell to Daimler and was transformed into an undistinguished middle-class sedan, and a badge-engineered one at that.

Even aspirants to the mass-production stakes suffered the fate of Durant. This was understandable – in a smaller market there was no room for any more contenders, and they picked medium-sized models when the public wanted something smaller. In such British hopefuls as

tended to boost Oldsmobile's then impressive sales by offering an up-market type of automobile listing around the $1,600 (£320) mark. Capacity was 4.2 litres, output 81 hp, and wheel-base 125 in (3.2 m) to the 1930 Oldsmobile's 113.5 in (2.88 m). The motor apart, mechanical elements were predictable, except that fuel was fed by mechanical pump to the Johnson dual-choke carburettor (c on the motor drawing below) instead of by the all-too-familiar vacuum system. One expected – and got – a three-speed unit transmission with central floor shift, a

single-plate clutch, internal-expanding mechanical four-wheel brakes (the contracting type was on its way out, even in the United States), and semi-elliptic springing. The engine was ingenious, no least of all in its construction; it was the first volume-production vee-eight to feature both banks of cylinders cast monobloc with the upper crankcase, an innovation usually credited to Ford. The carburation apart, the most intriguing feature of the 90-degree Viking eight wa its valve gear (a). Though of an L-head configuration, it featured horizontal

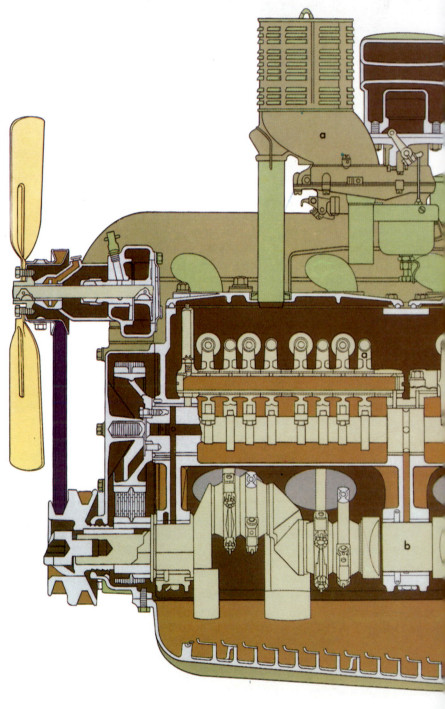

One might call the Oldsmobile Viking an unmitigated flop. It lasted only from April, 1929, until the autumn of 1930, few ventured outside its native United States, and only just over eight thousand attracted buyers. The Depression got there first. Views of the sedan (left and right) stamp it as unmistakably a late twenties design by General Motors, retaining wood wheels. The front end treatment with its V-badge (signifying a vee-eight motor as well as the Viking name) is especially reminiscent of Harley Earl's legendary 1929 La Salle, and in convertible guise Oldsmobile's companion make looks very like Cadillac's. But while the La Salle was conceived as a cheaper and lighter Cadillac, the Viking was in-

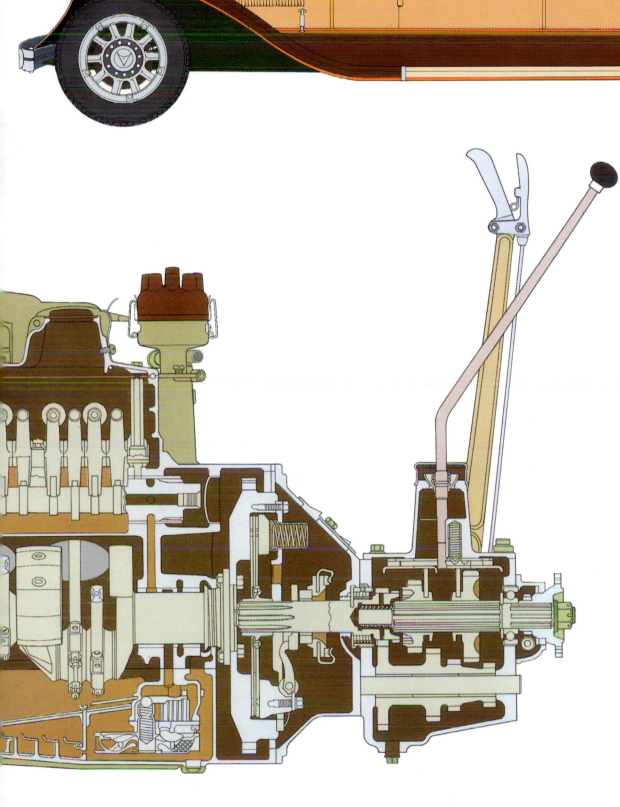

valves parallel with the ground, which gave a more efficient combustion chamber shape and were said to breathe as well as overhead valves. Where the system certainly scored was from the servicing standpoint, since valve adjustment called for no dismantling: the valves could be approached through cover plates within the vee. The three-main-bearing crankshaft (b) with 90-degree throws made for good balance. Nothing, alas, can save a fairly expensive middle-class car in a Depression, especially when it bears a new name. The Viking competed not only against the straight-eight Studebaker, the mid-range Chryslers, and the smaller Marmons, it also competed with the more expensive Buicks from the same parent firm. Buick, riding high at the nearly 200,000 units sold in 1929, tumbled to 119,000 in 1930. The Viking never got off the ground, and though General Motors's Oakland Division introduced a rather similar eight-cylinder engine design for 1931, this was Oakland's last year; the unit struggled on into 1932 as power for the more expensive of Pontiac's two lines, thereafter all General Motors's eights save the Cadillac's would preserve the inline configuration until 1949.

Angus-Sanderson, Bean, and Cubitt one can see the ancestors of 1948's Standard Vanguard, though they were killed off by the industrial unrest of 1920–21. By contrast, Clyno in England and Mathis in France were casualties of one and the same ambition – to beat the big battalions with insufficient capital. Clyno's Frank Smith consistently tried to match Morris's prices, and it killed his company in the end. The last straw was his bid for a £100 light car in 1928, something that even Morris would not achieve until three years later. In terms of sheer volume and survival, Emile Mathis fared rather better: his company was good for nearly twenty thousand units a year in 1927, and it kept going until 1935. It was, however, the same old story. Citroën's sales were a cool sixty thousand, and even he would run out of money when he tried to launch his new *traction* in 1934. Further, Citroën's exciting new experiment warranted a rescue bid from Michelin, whereas Mathis had nothing to offer save factory capacity. Thus, he suffered the same fate as a lesser rival, Jérome Donnet: he was bought up by foreign interests anxious to circumvent France's swingeing import duties. Donnet's plant made licence-built Fiats, and Mathis's Ford V8s. One cannot help adding an ironic postscript to show that the game of contraction never ends: Ford-France, hovering at the bottom of the first division in 1954, were snapped up by Simca, the erstwhile French Fiat operation. Ten years later, Simca, unable to fight unaided against the Big Three, were themselves absorbed by Chrysler International!

As for the assemblers, they fell by the wayside. At the 1923 London Show could be seen such native breeds as Airedale, Albatros, Autocrat, Bayliss-Thomas, Eric-Campbell, Eric-Longden, GWK, Hampton, Horstman, McKenzie, Marseal, Meteorite, NP, Seabrook, Turner, Waverley, Westcar, and Whitlock. Countless others could not even afford a stand. Most of them used such familiar components as Meadows or Coventry-Climax engines, and Moss gearboxes. Some had their engaging idiosyncrasies – GWK's friction drive or Horstman's kick starter – but none of them were at Olympia in 1931, even if a handful preserved a token existence. The Whitlock, for instance, had transformed itself from an over-priced 1.5-litre challenger to Morris to a rival for the expensive Lagondas in the 3-litre category, but it profited the car not at all. Lagonda themselves were in trouble but were to survive a receivership in 1935.

In other respects the picture was the same as in the United States. Only the ante was lower. Of the less expensive runners-up, Singer of Coventry were just about a viable operation in 1939, with a potential of maybe nine thousand cars a year. Of middle-class makers, Riley and Triumph kept out of the receiver's hands until the eve of the Second World War, while rearmament saved one German contemporary, Stoewer, from trouble. In France, Berliet and Unic survived thanks to their heavy diesel trucks.

There remains one further legacy of the 1920s – better roads. If Australia's bitumen was a Second World War phenomenon, and if the first of the American freeways – the Pennsylvania Turnpike, following the route of a disused railroad – did not open until October, 1940, there were earlier influences at work. Not, be it said, in Britain, where primitive bypasses (we would now dismiss them as "inner ring roads") represented the limit to which cheeseparing governments would go. Nor yet in Germany: in 1930, Adolf Hitler's Thousand Year Reich lay three years in the future.

Italy's *autostrade* had, however, been authorized in 1925, in the shape of preliminary stretches linking Milan and Cremona, and Brescia and Verona. Subsequent plans embraced all the country's major cities, and by 1932, 387 miles (623 km) of *autostrade* were open. Longest of the continuous runs was the 136-mile (219 km) stretch – Turin–Milan–Brescia.

Not all assembled cars were small and cheap. The London-built Whitlock (*centre*) had started as a copybook 1.5-litre Eleven, but by the end of the decade (the breed lasted into 1930–31), it had become a luxury competitor for Invicta, Lagonda, and Sunbeam, using the 3.3-litre valve-in-head Meadows six. Promoted as "The Six that Satisfies", it was hardly ever seen, albeit Whitlock fitted a radiator which might have been mistaken for a product of their more illustrious neighbours, Bentley Motors, also building cars in Cricklewood at that time. The big brake drums heightened the resemblance, but only about thirty 20/70 Whitlocks were sold.

The baby car of a past decade. In 1930, the Austin Seven was beginning to be old hat. Outside the United States, the splash-lubricated engine was *démodé*, and un-coupled four-wheel brakes were unacceptable everywhere. Austin, indeed, were just about to link all four wheels to the pedal and remove some of the more hazardous pleasures from 7-hp motoring, albeit a clutch with a pedal travel that felt a fraction of an inch was still with us and would be until the end in 1939. Herbert Austin's Baby was, nevertheless, the effective prototype of the modern miniature car, and in 1930, it was being built under licence in three foreign countries – the American Austin Co. of Butler, Pennsylvania, were launching a left-hook edition, Dixi of Eisenach (recently taken over

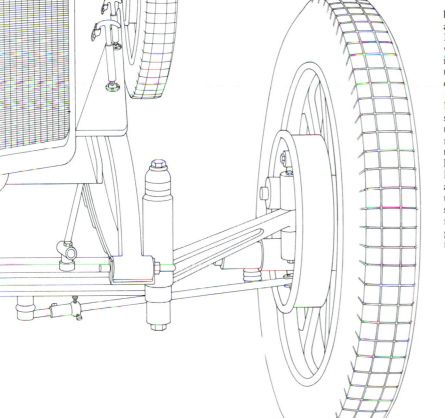

by BMW) handled German production, and Lucien Rosengart supplied the French market. Of these, the Rosengart was the least-publicized, yet stayed longest in the game, their 1952–53 Ariette retaining unmistakable traces of an Austin origin. Here is an early example from 1928–29: it's almost pure Baby Austin in a Rue de la Paix frock, even if the usual soup-plate wheel discs are missing from this roadster. The wide, ribbon-type radiator shell was very similar to that of the BMW-built Dixi, and the hood line is lower than a native Austin's. Prices paralleled those of the British prototype, at around the £110–120 ($550–600) mark, though despite a dealer chain in France said to be 2,500 strong, the little car never really caught on: Frenchmen wanted bigger cars like the 8CVs of Citroën and Renault. By 1931, the Rosengart was show

ing a greater degree of sophistication, with semi-elliptic springs at the rear, and the last pre-war 4CVs were quite stylish, if a little too like Simca's version of the Fiat Balilla in appearance. The company even essayed something that Austin was wise enough to avoid: a species of Gallic Wolseley Hornet using a 1,097-cc six-cylinder motor in a lengthened (but not reinforced) frame. This one had the refinement of vacuum-servo brakes, while Rosengart would later try to challenge Citroën with a front-wheel drive car built under German Adler licence. This failed: and though the company fared somewhat better (around a thousand units sold) with a sporty 2-litre *Supertraction* using 11CV Citroën mechanical elements, they reverted in the end to gallicized Baby Austins.

Though fully lit at night, these were not, initially at any rate, dual carriageways in the modern sense. Mussolini, however, made them self-financing by the imposition of tolls. Curiously, the foreign press was not wholly appreciative. A contemporary report lamented not only the "deadly monotony", but also "the comparatively moderate speed at which drivers travel over them". Maximum speed was, of course, cruising speed, but this particular observer was surprised to find that neither was much in excess of 40 mph (65 km/h).

His explanation was, nevertheless, the correct one. "There appears", the report continues, "to be a critical speed at which all cars become noisy, tiring to handle, and uncomfortable to ride in." This certainly applied to the ill-damped suspensions, rigidly-mounted engines, and low rev limits of the middle 1920s – and in Italy roads had anticipated car design. Jano's brilliant new overhead-camshaft Alfa Romeos and Vincenzo Lancia's Lambda were too expensive for the average Italian, who had to make do with small Fiats and Bianchis and the more austere species of Ansaldo. Hence, the 1930s would see a new generation of short-stroke, high-revving engines in small family sedans. And if Germany's more dramatic *Autobahn* network would breed some interesting exercises in aerodynamics and high gearing, the 1932 Shows would introduce the world to two of the outstanding small cars of the era, the Lancia Augusta and the 508 Fiat, even though the latter would not reach its full flowering until the advent of the *millecento* version (Type 508C) in 1937.

To summarize the *autostradale* influence, let us take a look back to 1930 and the 514. In seven years, cylinder capacity had been substantially reduced – from 1,438 to 1,089 cc. Also down was weight – from just over 2,200 lb (1,000 kg) to a mere 1,874 lb (850 kg). The Millecento was more compact, measuring only 13 ft 3 in (4.05 m) from stem to stern. First-class hydraulic brakes and sophisticated suspension were only to be expected, but whereas a 514 would work laboriously up to 55 mph (90 km/h) and cruise at 45 mph (75 km/h), a good 508C would exceed 70 mph (115 km/h) and could be held at 65 mph (105 km/h) all day. Better still, its motorway-inspired aerodynamics, if not as spectacular as some of its German contemporaries, permitted a fuel consumption in the region of 35 mpg (8 lit/100).

Not all the concomitants of "pure transportation" were dull.

The extreme in the bespoke. Duesenberg made precisely 470 cars between 1929 and the end in 1937, and nothing cost less than $13,500 (£2,700) even in the United States. Though there were factory-approved bodies, a run of forty of any individual style was exceptional, while by 1935, when this SJ Airflow Coupé was built, fabric as a body rather than a top covering had been obsolete for four years.

A one-off by Bohman and Schwartz of Pasadena, this one reputedly set its owner back more than twenty grand (say £4,000). The rear seats had to be of opera type owing to the restricted headroom, and chromium plating was, exceptionally, limited to bumpers, hubcaps, and radiator shell. Even the side panels of the hood — usually cluttered up with assorted brightwork – are uncommonly restrained.

2

PAINLESS SOPHISTCATION

The last ten years of peace were years of transition. At heart, this transition was sociological rather than technical. The automobile was at last emerging for good from its initial role as a rich man's plaything. Women drivers, hitherto a rarity outside the United States, were becoming more numerous in other countries; hence, engineering departments had to work still harder in the painkilling department than they had done in the 1920s. Pressure lubrication, coils, cellulose, and chromium plate were not enough.

As we have seen, mass production was by no means unknown in Europe. By the end of the 1920s, Citroën, Peugeot, Renault, and Mathis in France, Opel in Germany, Fiat in Italy, and Austin, Morris, and Standard in England were capable of substantial annual outputs. Typical figures for 1929, the last pre-Depression season, were Morris, 63,522 units, Fiat, 42,780, and Opel, 34,578. These might be a drop in the bucket beside Ford's 1.5 million and Chevrolet's 950,000. They could not even match the 92,034 turned out by Chrysler, a strictly middle-class make – comparable European breeds in this price-class would have been content with a mere 10,000. There was no doubt, however, which way the wind was blowing. Even in 1932, Fiat, with one of Europe's weakest home markets behind them, managed to sell nearly 20,000 cars, of which over half stayed in Italy.

Labour might still be cheap, but capital was scarce. Therefore, to stay in the game, one had to turn out plenty of standardized vehicles in the cheapest possible way. The rat race had, however, not reached the alarming proportions to be encountered in the 1950s; a small maker with no particular *cachet* (Singer in England, for instance, or La Licorne in France) could get by on annual sales well below the ten thousand mark. Volvo of Sweden, who were on the way up, were as yet virtually unknown outside Scandinavia, yet with the aid of a healthy truck business they managed happily on a mere two or three thousand passenger cars a year. Economic stringency did, however, tend to produce too many restatements of warmed-over American themes, even if these showed themselves at their worst in the styling department. It also delayed the adoption of such progressive ideas as unitary construction and all-independent springing, which would have involved retooling on a formidable scale. It is worth remembering that, in 1932, it cost the Chrysler Corporation $9 million to convert the Plymouth engine plant from four- to six-cylinder types; hence, there was an alarming tendency to "change the colour of the upholstery and call it next year's model!". Despite the fiercely competitive tenor of the market, even the biggest firms worked on a two to three-year design cycle, ringing the changes on mechanical and styling improvements. The American Fords of 1933

and 1934 were virtually identical in both mechanical and styling departments, while Morris's major chassis and body changes announced during the summer of 1935 were not complemented by an engine redesign until the 1938 model year.

The world was edging gingerly into the motorway age. France's *routes nationales* might still be much as Napoleon I left them, and Britain might be wedded to perilous three-lane highways barely adequate to the 40 mph (65 km/h) cruising speeds to which her citizens were addicted, but the Italian *autostrade* were already a *fait accompli*, and the first German *Autobahnen* would be opened in 1935. Before the United States entered the Second World War, she would have her Pennsylvania Turnpike, herald of the coming freeway system. Thus, to the economic parameters that faced a designer in our period was added the need for a car capable of cruising at a sustained 60 mph (100 km/h) without either becoming airborne or showering reciprocating parts all over the road.

The state of the art in 1930 was not vastly different from that of 1920. The game had its rules, and the rules themselves were governed, as they had been for more than thirty years, by the *système* Panhard – a water-cooled engine with vertical cylinders mounted at the front of a chassis frame and driving the rear wheels through the medium of a friction clutch and a selective, sliding-type gearbox. Bevel-type rear axles predominated, and the suspension consisted of a leaf spring at each of the corners.

This covered almost every car on the market. Twin-cylinder power units, admittedly, were found in a few cyclecar hangovers and subutility models such as the British Jowett. Tatra in Czechoslovakia and Franklin in the United States preferred air cooling. Rear-engined cars cropped up from time to time – from the austere little Hanomag Kommissbrot recently retired from production in Germany to the aeroplane-fuselage shape of the costly straight-eight Burney Streamline (one of these latter had lately been commissioned by the heir to the British throne). Lancia of Italy built not only chassis-less cars but threw in independently-sprung front wheels as well, while the German Röhr boasted independent rear suspension into the bargain. On some British Alvises and American Cords and Ruxtons, the engine drove the front wheels. Peugeot followed the example of many a heavy-truck maker, preferring worm to bevel drive for their rear axles. These exceptions, nevertheless, served principally to prove the rule. "Putting the works up one end" still represented rank heresy, and any French designer would have been deeply shocked had he been informed that within less than half a century not a single model produced in the *système* Panhard's homeland would conform to the dictates of that system.

The Franklin Airman Sedan (*centre left*) of 1930. The heresies of the air-cooled Franklin were concealed beneath an orthodox exterior and had been since 1925, when Ralph Hamlin, the Los Angeles distributor, threatened to cancel his agency if the car wasn't given a "radiator" that looked like everyone else's. The result was elegant, especially when clothed with one of Franklin's exotic "factory customs", pleasing if hardly economic to offer once production fell below four thousand a year. The steering wheel spider (*bottom*) reflected Herbert Franklin's credo of "scientific light weight", being of aluminium. Bakelite was likewise replacing wood on rims. The six-cylinder Franklin engine (*opposite, bottom*) is immediately identifiable by its separate "pots" and by the huge sirocco fan keyed to the nose of the crankshaft. The shroud directed the air down a duct to the top of the cylinders, whence it passed downwards through the medium of steel or copper fins. The small oil tank alongside the fan supplies lubricant to the valve rockers. Clutch and transmission are the usual copybook American, though Franklin didn't adopt four-wheel brakes until 1928, and all their cars save the last vee-twelves and the cut-price Olympics featured wooden frames and full-elliptic springing.

True, there had been some significant advances. If full electrics had been *de rigueur* everywhere by 1922 at the latest, the need to cater for a broader, unmechanically-minded public had recently led to the abandonment of the magneto in favour of the coil and battery. Only sports and luxury models still clung to the older arrangement; on the latter, this tended to serve as a supplementary ignition. Four-wheel brakes, a sensation of the 1919 Shows, were now universal practice, even Ford and Chevrolet having surrendered to modernity on their 1928 models. With four-wheel brakes had come the balloon tyre, but the only other fundamental mechanical change had been the adoption of the silent, helical-bevel rear axle, which eliminated the endemic growlings of many an early-vintage machine. It was unkindly said that, on the cheaper axles of the 1930s, some warning of impending collapse was needed! (The old straight-bevel axles growled most of the time, whereas, on the later types, growls and whines were warnings of approaching trouble.)

In other respects, however, the period's major developments were aesthetic, cosmetic, and concerned with creature comforts.

Catering for the laity, who understood neither the Otto cycle nor the functions of a clutch, presented headaches in itself, even without the attentions of a cost accountant. Engines, admittedly, were now generally reliable and needed no drastic attention. It was not until the spread of motorways in the 1960s, for instance, that it became almost mandatory to endow an inline four-cylinder power unit with five robust main bearings instead of the three that were general practice in the 1930s –

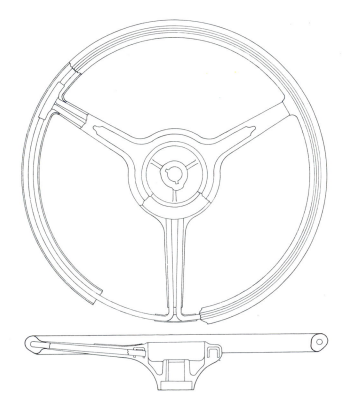

Two by General Motors – and one out-sider. The origins of the 1937 Chevrolet (*opposite, top right*) and 1931 Opel (*right*) are unmistakable, though six years separate them. Chevrolet were, of course, long-standing advocates of upstairs valves on their splash-lubricated motors. By 1937, we have such amenities as coil-spring independent front suspension, synchromesh, hydraulic brakes, and hypoid back axles, none of them to be encountered on the German car. In any case, Europe's harsher fiscal climate and higher fuel prices called for a smaller and more frugal six than the Chevrolet, which ran to 3.2 litres even in 1931. The flat-head Opel disposed of 1.8 litres and 32 hp, and it was probably more automobile than the average German could afford to run. The company did well to sell over thirty thousand in three seasons. Finally, as a total contrast, the 1936 1½-litre Riley Adelphi sedan (*opposite, top left*). Here, the sole American influence is in the integral rear trunk with its external access. The rest of it is one hundred per cent British: handbuilt wood-framed coachwork, centre-lock wire wheels, a high-efficiency overhead-valve four-cylinder hemi-head engine, and a four-speed Wilson pre-selective transmission. In standard form, 70 mph (112 km/h) were about the limit, but its price of £350 ($1,750) matched the local figure for a Master Chevrolet fairly closely, and by buying British you saved £9 ($45) a year in circulation tax.

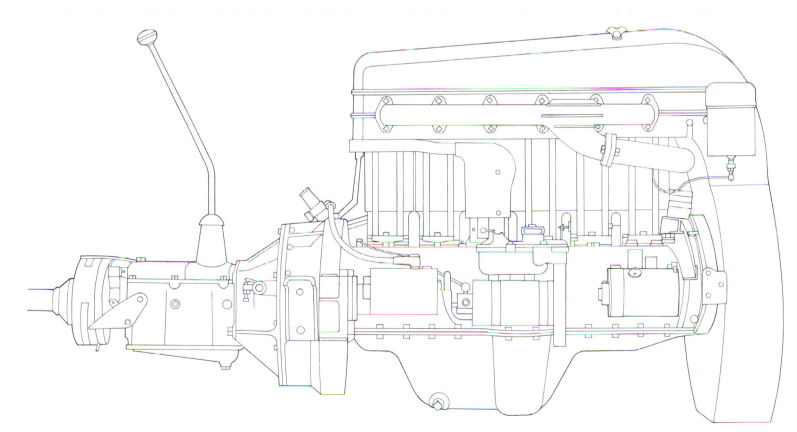

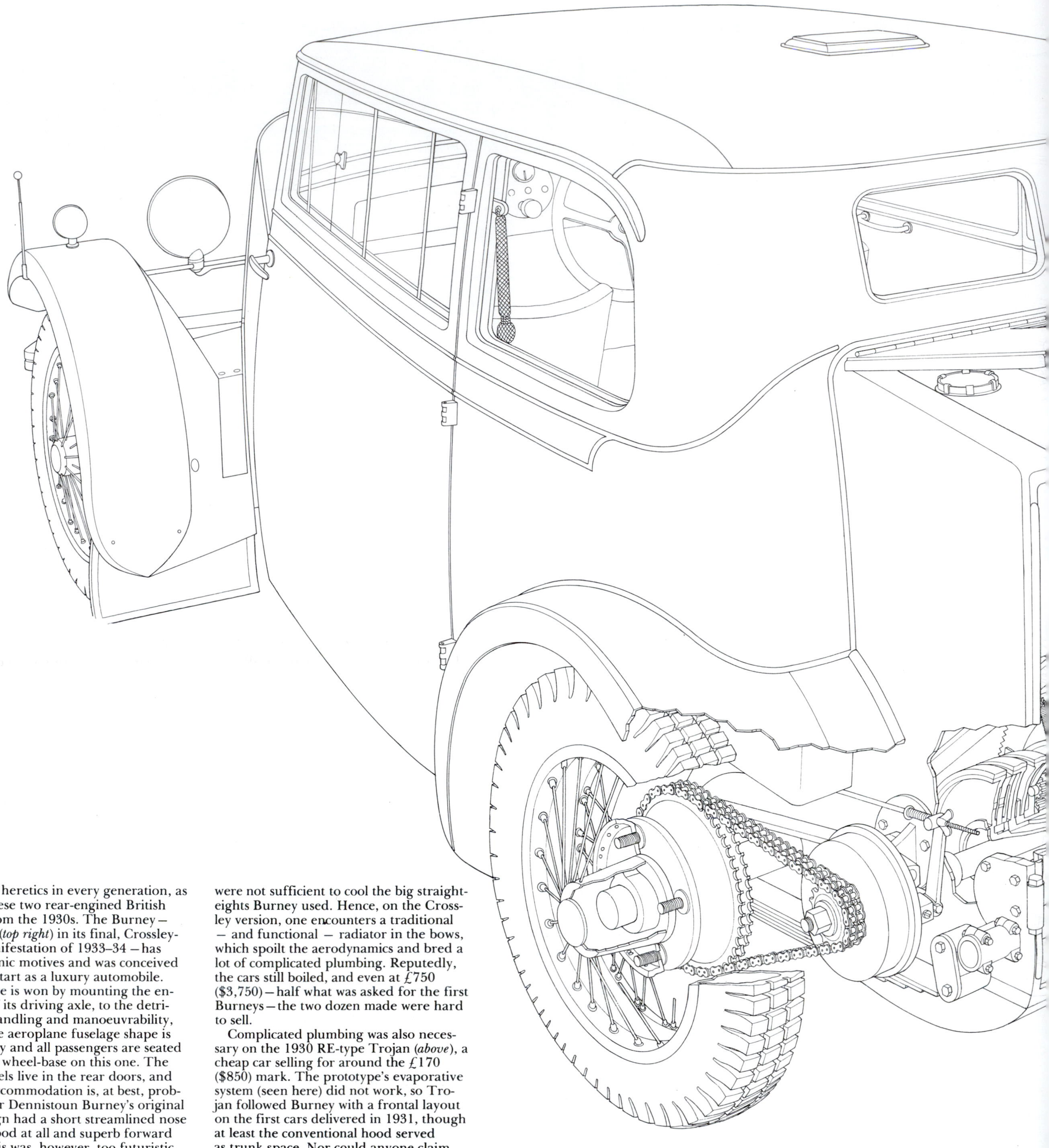

There are heretics in every generation, as witness these two rear-engined British layouts from the 1930s. The Burney — here seen (*top right*) in its final, Crossley-made manifestation of 1933–34 — has aerodynamic motives and was conceived from the start as a luxury automobile. Extra space is won by mounting the engine aft of its driving axle, to the detriment of handling and manoeuvrability, though the aeroplane fuselage shape is noteworthy and all passengers are seated within the wheel-base on this one. The spare wheels live in the rear doors, and luggage accommodation is, at best, problematic. Sir Dennistoun Burney's original 1930 design had a short streamlined nose with no hood at all and superb forward vision. This was, however, too futuristic for the public of those days, while the ear-type lateral radiators alongside the engine were not sufficient to cool the big straight-eights Burney used. Hence, on the Crossley version, one encounters a traditional — and functional — radiator in the bows, which spoilt the aerodynamics and bred a lot of complicated plumbing. Reputedly, the cars still boiled, and even at £750 ($3,750) — half what was asked for the first Burneys — the two dozen made were hard to sell.

Complicated plumbing was also necessary on the 1930 RE-type Trojan (*above*), a cheap car selling for around the £170 ($850) mark. The prototype's evaporative system (seen here) did not work, so Trojan followed Burney with a frontal layout on the first cars delivered in 1931, though at least the conventional hood served as trunk space. Nor could anyone claim that the RE was futuristic: this astounding automobile resembled a sporty

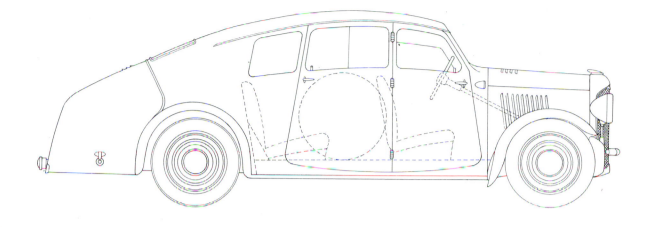

fabric sedan of the period, with its semi-cycle fenders and rounded vee-radiator. Nothing was, however, the way it looked, as the drawing shows. The vertical four-cylinder two-cycle motor drove forward by roller chain to the axle via a three-speed epicyclic transmission, and (incredibly) there were no brakes on the front wheels, even in 1935, the RE's last season. Unlike the original Trojan, a rustic automobile which could climb anything on which the wheels could get a grip, the RE was nobody's favourite. It was overweight, underpowered, and tended to boil on hills. In any case, a cruising speed of 37 mph (60 km/h) and a maximum of 45 (72 km/h) were no longer adequate, even in Britain. Not much more than a hundred REs found buyers. Thereafter, Trojan, though still loyal to the two-cycle motor, confined their efforts to light trucks.

smaller Fiats and Singers, indeed, continued to manage with two. Rates of rotation, though going up, remained modest. The average 1930 American engine developed its maximum output at around 3,200 rpm, at which speed simple splash lubrication sufficed for Chevrolet, Ford, and Hudson, among others. Pressure systems had, however, long been general practice in Europe. Even in 1939, 4,000 rpm represented an acceptable limit on a touring car, albeit one important by-product of *Autobahn* influence was the narrowing of stroke-bore ratios. We have already encountered the small Fiats of the 1920s, but they remain classic examples of the way things were going. The company's standard small car of 1929, the 509A, had cylinder dimensions of 2.24 × 3.82 in (57 × 97 mm), and as the machine was overbodied and undergeared, it was revving its heart out at 50–55 mph (80–90 km/h). Its 1938 counterpart of only slightly greater capacity but shorter stroke – 2.68 × 2.95 in (68 × 75 mm) – developed half as many brake horses at 4,400 rpm and carried four people at an easy 70 mph (115 km/h). As for the 6,000 rpm commonplace in modern 1,100-cc sedans, this would have been acceptable only on the racing circuits, and beyond both the metallurgical and sound-damping capabilities of any maker. It is also fair to say that the necessary quality of tyres and fuel for the fulfilment of the ensuing performance would also have been unthinkable in 1939 – or in 1949, for that matter.

More power was certainly available: 20–22 bhp a litre was commonplace at the beginning of our decade, but even "cooking" engines would be good for an honest 30 bhp by 1940. By this time, too, there was a marked swing from side valves to the greater efficiency of pushrod-operated overhead valves. This was, however, as far as the average volume producer would venture. Upstairs camshafts with their chain or gear drives were considered too noisy for family sedans and too expensive for the cost accountants. The sophisticated valve gears of Riley (pushrods, twin high-set camshafts, and hemispherical combustion chambers), Singer (single overhead camshaft), and Salmson (twin overhead camshafts) were not copied by rivals. Morris and Fiat tried overhead camshafts and then retreated in the face of costing and maintenance problems. Even in the rarefied realm of the luxury car, the

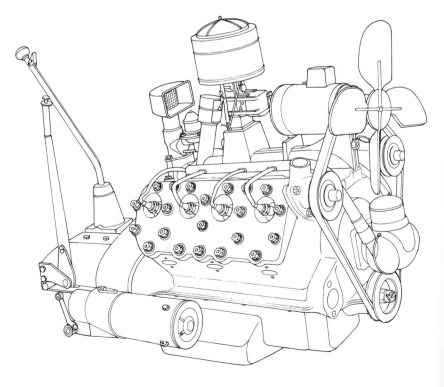

The rear-engined 150H Mercedes-Benz (*top*) is an oddity of 1934–35, and a forgotten one at that. Only 25 were made, though at least 6,500 of the touring 130H and 170H sedans and cabrio-limousines found buyers between 1934 and 1939. This odd creature resembled a long-tailed, notchback Volkswagen, though the engine was a water-cooled L-head four and hung over the rear "axle" at the end of a central backbone frame with all-independent suspension. Hatch space under the short hood (*bottom left*) was very limited, and a standard suitcase just would not

fit, so the manufacturers offered a special fitted suitcase.

Ford's legendary 221-cu. in. (3,622 cc) flathead vee-eight engine (*bottom right*). V for voluminous body space and for less space wasted on the engine. This was used by Ford's overseas operations as well as by the parent factory, between 1932 and 1942, and after the Second World War as well. The vee-eight gave the power of eight cylinders from a unit that had the length of a four-cylinder engine, though on a wide-angle unit (90 degrees) like the

Ford, it was not really viable to use the same chassis as for a four-cylinder car, even if Ford did just that in 1932 and 1933.

Two essays in compactness, the 1930 Lancia Lambda with vee-four engine (*top*) and the 1935 German Ford with vee-eight engine (*centre*), and one car that demonstrates the straight-eight of the period — "an automobile of which at least half the length is hood" — the Horch 853A of 1938 (*bottom*).

Lancia's Lambda had the ultimate in compact power units, a vee-four with an angle of only 13 degrees between banks, and a block only 22 in (56 cm) long. Thus, despite the fact that the company did not use a unit gearbox, a very large proportion of the available wheel-base length (122 in or 3.23 m in the case of short-chassis cars) could be used for bodywork. This also made long-chassis cars very long indeed: even tourers could seat eight.

Once one had left the engine behind, Ford engineering was uninspiring. The three-speed synchromesh transmission was common to virtually every other American car, brakes were mechanical, and suspension was the classical Ford transverse-leaf type at both ends, admirable for assaults on muddy tracks and ploughed fields, but terribly bouncy elsewhere. The short wheel-base (112 in or 2.8 m) did not help either, though on the 1935 line they moved the engine over the front axle, thus sacrificing the elegance of the earlier Model-40 in favour of more body space and rear seats within the

wheel-base. Differences between native and foreign strains of the Ford V8 (the car was also made in Britain, France, and Australia, as well as Germany) were mainly stylistic, rather than mechanical, though cars of entirely German or British origin retained mechanical brakes up to the outbreak of the Second World War. Only the practised eye can tell that this car comes from Cologne, rather than from Dearborn, Dagenham, Poissy, or Geelong.

Horch were wedded to eight-cylinder engines and made nothing else from 1926 to 1939, apart from a handful of prohibitively expensive vee-twelves. Significantly, though, they chose the more compact type of power unit for their middle-class line. During the same period, they turned out between three and four thousand straight-eights, the "sporting" 853 series (shown here) accounting for a round thousand of them. The 4.9-litre ten-bearing single overhead-camshaft engine, developed in 1930–31 by Fiedler and Schleicher to replace a less-than-satisfactory twin-camshaft unit, gave only 120 hp, and on a car like this, it was hardly reasonable to expect more than 80 mph (130 km/h). Nor did one get it. Most cars later than 1935 had the transverse-leaf independent front suspension, shown here (*bottom left*) on the smaller and relatively inexpensive 830B of 1937, and semi-elliptic leaf springs at the rear. However, up to the end, in 1939, some Horchs (usually long-chassis limousines) were still being delivered with beam axles at both ends.

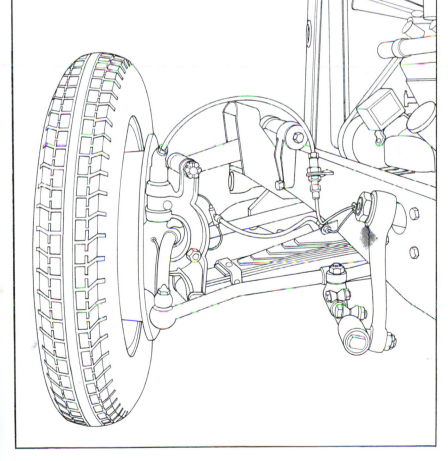

The 7.1-litre sleeve-valve Daimler engine (*right*) announced at the 1926 Shows served as the prototype for the company's twelve-cylinder units marketed up to 1935 and was truly a Double Six. Here, the twin water pumps (*a*), magnetos (*b*), and distributors (*c*) are visible, but the engine also had an individual four-jet carburettor for each block of cylinders. The engine gave 150 bhp at 2,480 rpm and needed to do so, since a chassis alone weighed over two tons, making limousines on the longest 163-in (4.1 m) wheel-base three-tonners. Incredibly, a sports chassis with underslung frame was marketed in 1930, but even on the 150-in (3.8 m) wheel-base, its appearance was almost a parody of classic themes, with 7 ft (2.1 m), no less, of hood. Five mpg (56 lit/100) on petrol and 350 mpg on lubricating oil meant that Double Sixes were for the wealthiest citizens only.

More cylinders mean flexibility, silence, and freedom from audible power impulses, but it is easy to see from this 1931 Maybach DS8 Zeppelin (*below* and *opposite*) why better sound-damping methods were

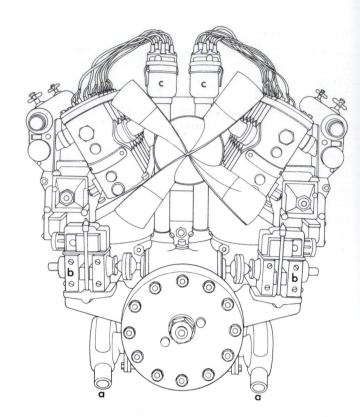

so welcome. Of 8 litres' capacity, the pushrod overhead-valve Maybach developed 200 bhp. Mounting the blocks at 60 degrees made for a fairly compact width, but length was another matter: a 4-litre six, after all, is quite long. The motor used every inch of space under a hood that was 7 ft (2.1 m) long, which explains why not a few Maybach hoods employed full-length lifting handles. Note the centrally mounted camshaft (*a*), the individual dual-choke carburettor (*b*) for each bank of cylinders, and the massive eight-bearing crankshaft (*c*). Even with liberal use of light alloys — the block was of silumin — the motor alone weighed 1,100 lb (just över 500 kg), or not much less than a Fiat 126 of our own times. A complete Zeppelin could turn the scales at close on 8,400 lb (3,800 kg). With prices that could run up as high as $40,000 (the equivalent of £8,000 then) in the United States, sales were understandably modest: probably not more than three hundred twelve-cylinder Maybachs of all types in ten years. Not shown here is perhaps the oddest aspect of the design — the transmission.

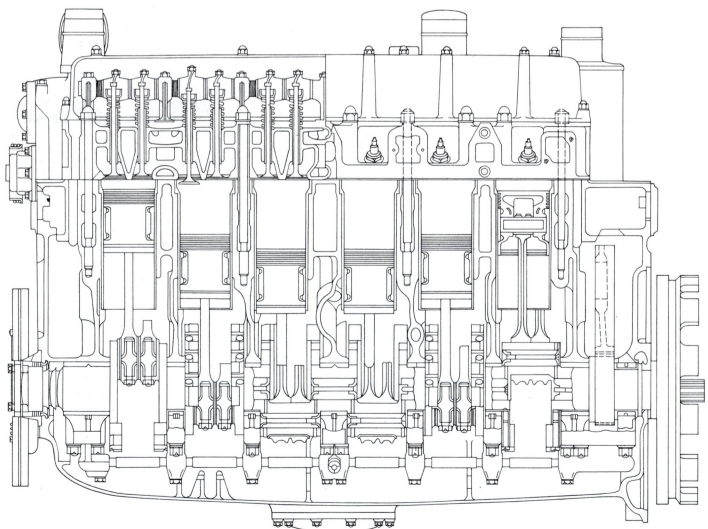

German Horch, which entered our period with a twin overhead-camshaft power unit, soon converted to the simpler single-camshaft layout. In any case, the development of high-octane fuels essential to greater mechanical sophistication was delayed by the Second World War. In Britain, the short-stroke unit was also delayed by the War, as well as by an unenlightened fiscal policy which took into consideration only the bore of the cylinders.

As to ancillaries, gravity feed still had its adherents, but the complexities of the vacuum system caused the simpler mechanical pump, by now universal in the United States, to gain ground fast elsewhere. Electric pumps, though favoured in mountainous countries owing to their relative freedom from air locks, were too complicated for the new generation of motorists, though the Nuffield Group in England adopted them successfully from 1932 onwards, and sold SU systems (made by one of their subsidiaries, Skinner Union) to a number of other British firms, notably Rover and SS. A captive source can be an excellent motivation, and the SU pump worked well, though over-electrification can present problems in the case of a flat battery.

Sheer power was, of course, secondary to smoothness and flexibility, and in this department the standardization of rubber engine mounts was perhaps the most important step. This improvement was not, however, universally accepted until 1933–34, and in the meantime, other aids to flexibility had to be explored.

The obvious aid – and one that had been prevalent on and off since 1904 – was more cylinders. Sixes and eights had been on the up-grade since 1926, and the trend continued well into the 1930s.

The compact vee-eight was never wholly acceptable. Its uneven firing characteristics led to an irritating "wuffle", large-scale manufacture called for costly tooling, and it took the almost unlimited resources of Ford to master the technique of mass monobloc casting. Europeans, fiscally discouraged from really big runs of anything larger than a 3-litre, left this type alone. Hence, its vogue in the 1930s was confined to two of the American giants: Ford and the Cadillac Division of General Motors.

The straight-eight proved more popular until the Depression really took hold; it appealed aesthetically as well as technically, as long hoods were all the rage in 1930. Further, firms with shaky budgets and anxious shareholders could purchase proprietary units of this type from Lycoming or Continental, a state of affairs which explains the formidable line-up of eights fielded by Weimar Germany at the peak of

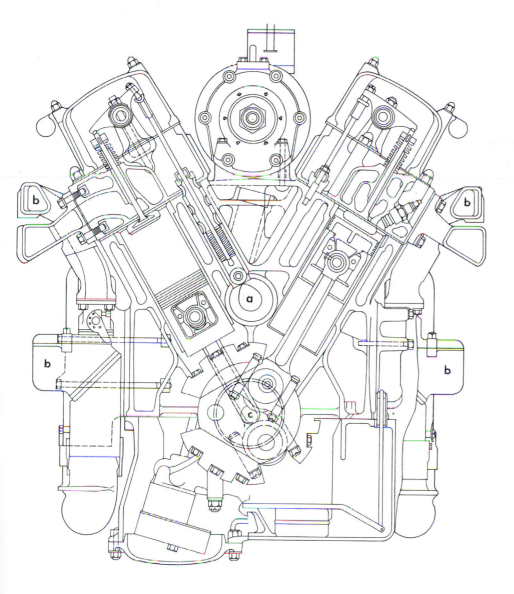

Outside the realm of the sports car it is an accepted axiom that the bigger an engine and the greater the number of cylinders, the fewer forward speeds are required. Not so Karl Maybach: though content with a two-speed-and-reverse affair on Model T Ford lines for his first, relatively modest 5.7-litre six way back in 1922, he had progressed by 1931 to the fearsome dual-range *Doppelschnellgang*, which offered eight forward and four reverse speeds at the cost, understandably, of some duplication of ratios. (*Above*) The attractive badge on the twelve-cylinder Maybach.

Sedans of the 1930s. The 1933 Vauxhall Light Six (*top left*) and 1934 Austin Light 12/4 Harley (*bottom*) are typical early thirties specimens with compound curves in evidence, especially around the forepeak. If the Austin's shape suggests other models, both British and German, then it is a direct consequence of Budd influence from the new presswork plants in Oxford and Berlin. The 1936 Renault Primaquatre (*centre left*) reflects American influences from a year or so before and utilizes the full width of the frame to make a six-seater out of a compact car. More interesting, though, is its famed flathead "85" motor of 2,383 cc, with four cylinders where one would still expect six. Rough it might be, but it was also tough and still fitted to light trucks seventeen years later. The 1939 Lagonda (*centre right*) and 1937 Lincoln Zephyr (*right*) represent two approaches to the twelve-cylinder automobile, though curiously, it is the expensive British car, at £1,600 or $8,000, that is the more sophisticated, with independently-sprung front wheels and hydraulic brakes. Fractionally bigger than the Lincoln – 4,480 cc as against 4,387 – it gave 158 hp to the American car's 113 – and needed to, since a sedan weighed over two tons and 100 mph (160 km/h) was already the norm for the *grande*

routière class. The semi-unitary Lincoln, as a Ford product, was still wedded to beam axles, transverse suspension, and mechanical brakes. The product-image called for the extra four cylinders, not the best thing from the maintenance standpoint, but between 1936 and 1948, the Zephyr family became what will probably be the best-selling twelve-cylinder line of all time. And for $1,190 (£238 at par), the combination of 90 mph (145 km/h) and 20 mpg (13.5 lit/100) couldn't be bad news.

Complication was the price of silence and smoothness in their ultimate form, though it is rather surprising to find Cadillac with a *new* sixteen-cylinder engine (*right*) as late as 1938. That it didn't sell (some five hundred were made in three seasons) was due as much to the "Little Recession" as to anything else, as it was a brilliant piece of work. With side-by-side valves for simplicity (and no worries on account of bulk) the engineers chose a wide 135-degree angle which allowed room for carburettors and manifolding within the vee. One distributor and one carburettor per bank of cylinders also made sense: treating it as two eights made it easier for mechanics. The result, though not much down on piston displacement, came out shorter and lighter than the original 1930 overhead-valve version, thus the theoretical loss of 15 hp mattered not at all. Unkind folk who dismissed the new flathead as "a lump of iron" had also forgotten that, in the era of alligator hoods, only those who worked on the engine got a clear view of it.

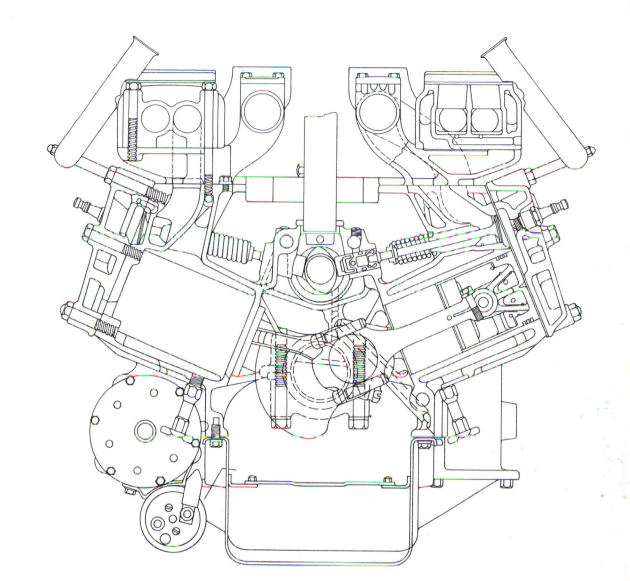

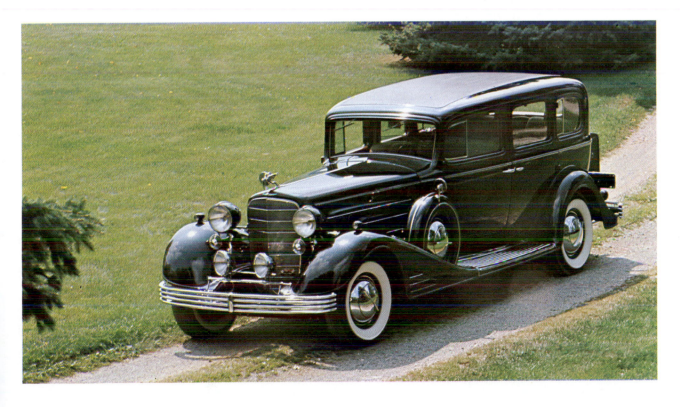

By contrast, this overhead-valve Cadillac Sixteen town car (*left*) of 1933, with Fleetwood coachwork, was cosmetic every inch of it, epitomizing the damn-the-cost Classicism which survived even into the years of *Brother, Can You Spare A Dime?* True, new stylistic evidences can be seen – the real radiator is hidden behind a vee-grille, the shell is painted, and even Cadillacs now had the fashionable fender skirts. The engine gave 165 hp from 7.4 litres, a three-speed synchromesh transmission was standard from the start in 1930, and with reasonably light bodywork, 95 mph (152 km/h) were possible. One didn't buy such a car for speed, though: the long wheel-base ran to 149 inches (3.8 m), even a simple sedan weighed over 5,000 lb (say 2,270 kg), and for 1933, Cadillac deliberately made their Sixteen exclusive, rationing the season's quota to 500 units. In those depressed times, however, they were lucky to sell 125.

49

the boom. Hansa and Simson – and probably several others – bought their units "off the peg" from Continental.

For those who insisted on the ultimate, there were vee-twelves and vee-sixteens; despite 1932's breadlines, American industry offered six distinct and different Twelves and two Sixteens (Marmon and Cadillac) that year. The price of undetectable power impulses and 0–100 mph in top gear was two of everything: on Daimler's Double Six each bank of cylinders had its own water pump, carburettor, and ignition arrangements. To this could be added prodigious thirsts: most of the big Americans averaged 9 mph (30 lit/100), and the Daimler was even worse. In any case, better sound-damping, independent wheel suspension, and, above all, aids to shifting would render such drastic measures superfluous by 1936, though Cadillac's Sixteen survived into 1940, along with the Twelves of Lincoln, Rolls-Royce, Lagonda, and Maybach. Mercedes-Benz had a new 6-litre vee-twelve on the stocks as well.

In passing, it can be mentioned that a major casualty of the new aids to silence was the sleeve-valve Knight engine, a sensation of 1909, and pursued energetically for several years in most of the major automobile-manufacturing countries of the world. Daimler led the British contingent and Willys was the American licencee, but other important firms in this field were Minerva of Belgium, Mercedes in Germany, and Panhard and Voisin in France. Silent it certainly was, and in early days, the fact that "it improved with use" cut down servicing costs in that it seldom required decarbonization. On the debit side were complexity, the expensive consequences of seizure, and a fearsome oil consumption which revealed itself in trailing plumes of blue smoke. By the beginning of our decade, Mercedes had already abdicated, Willys would quit in 1933, and Daimler two years later. The remaining loyalists – Minerva, Panhard, and Voisin – retained the Knight engine to the end simply because they could not afford to retool, albeit Voisin, in desperation, fitted their 1939 models with imported side-valve Graham units from the United States.

The trend towards the multi-cylinder engine reflected itself in the lower echelons of the market. By 1929, the 2-litre six was commonplace, and the 1930–35 period would see a brief craze (largely, though not exclusively, based in Britain) for real miniatures such as the 1.2-litre Triumph Scorpion and the 1.3-litre Wolseley Hornet. Such cars could accelerate smoothly away from 6 mph (10 km/h) in top, but on axle ratios of around 6:1, valve bounce was liable to set in well short of 60 mph (95–100 km/h). Their main interest to us is to reveal the cost accountancy school of engineering at its worst; such models were evolved by taking the frame of a small four and lengthening it without reinforcement to accommodate the two extra cylinders!

Just as better chassis engineering relegated the multi-barrelled giants to the super-luxury market, so also did it weed out the pint-sized sixes in favour of a new generation of fours. By the end of the 1930s, the big four was back again. In the United States, of course, the struggling Willys concern had long centred its energies on its 2.2-litre side-valve unit, known to every Allied serviceman of 1941 as the power behind the Jeep, but newcomers of 1936–37 were the 2,383-cc Renault 85, the 2,406-cc Stoewer Sedina, and Riley's classic Sixteen of very similar capacity. In 1939, sixes of less than 2 litres' capacity were once again in the minority.

The Wolseley Hornet and the sixteen-cylinder Cadillac, though poles apart in every other respect, were both attempts to solve the age-old headache of shifting gears. An enthusiast would use his box to capacity, extracting 15,000 miles (say 25,000 km) from even the primitive brake-lining material of the 1920s by keeping his foot off the brake pedal. The Smiths of the United States and Britain, the Duponts of France, and the

Schwartzes of Germany detested cog-swaps and never fully mastered the gentle art of the double-clutch. "Hanging on" to a high ratio was commonplace among elderly drivers even in the 1950s. The writer recalls a hair-raising run across Hampshire's Portsdown Hills in a Land-rover conducted by a retired chauffeur, who engaged third on leaving the city limits of Portsmouth and held it, restarts included, for the next thirty miles! Hence, much effort was devoted to alleviating the sufferings of such folk – and their cars.

The American philosophy, of course, centred round a big, lazy engine that did all its work in direct drive. The British, resigned to road conditions which demanded four forward speeds and liberal use of them all, were more concerned with painless shifting. Between them, however, the two English-speaking nations made the running in gearbox development between the years 1930 and 1940, just as France, Germany, and Italy introduced the everyday motorist to proper handling.

Synchromesh, first seen on 1929's Cadillacs and La Salles, offered truly clash-proof gears and freedom from the double-clutch technique. Initially confined to the two upper ratios (even where four speeds were specified), the system was all but universal in the United States by 1932, in which year it spread first to Britain and then to the rest of Europe. Few makers, of course, bothered to apply it to bottom gear (the Americans, indeed, would not do so until the middle sixties); this was an expensive luxury, especially at a time when this ratio tended to be suitable only for funeral processions. Alvis and the German ZF firm had effective all-synchromesh transmissions by 1934, but Hillman's version, a novelty of 1935, became a casualty of 1938's "little recession". Nobody noticed. Properly-spaced ratios were, sadly, reserved for the better sports cars. British four-speeders all too often suffered from "three bottoms and one top"; on Italian designs first gear was clearly intended for assaults on the vertical; and the short-lived four-speed transmissions tried in the United States between 1929 and 1933 featured two fairly high and close ratios (normal top and traffic top), a second which approximated to the normal first, and another example of the Italian-style crawler.

In the early 1930s, there was a short vogue for that economy device, the free wheel, which was often accompanied by an automatic clutch. The consequence was painless shifting at the price of loss of engine braking. Another refinement, though no novelty (Rolls-Royce had used it in 1907), was overdrive, in effect an auxiliary unit which furnished an extra cruising ratio for highway work, while holding the revs down. On early systems selection tended to be fully automatic; not a very desirable arrangement, since flooring the accelerator pedal automatically restored direct drive. On the majority of American cars so equipped the extra ratio was operative only in top, but at the other end of the spectrum was Maybach's fearsome *Doppelschnellgang* with its eight forward and four reverse ratios, hardly necessary on the elephantine automobiles produced by the Friedrichshafen concern. (This one, incidentally, was made available to other manufacturers and was actually taken up briefly by Lagonda in Britain and Walter in Czechoslovakia). By contrast, the American Auburn and the French Voisin favoured two-speed rear axles, already common practice in the truck world and used by Cadillac as early as 1914; these gave six or eight forward speeds, according to the type of main transmission.

Synchromesh was, of course, tailor-made for Britain's road conditions, and the majority of the country's major manufacturers had adopted it by 1934. A more peculiarly British answer to the shifting problem was, however, the Wilson preselective gearbox, first offered on 1929's larger Armstrong Siddeley models. It was, admittedly, a three-pedal affair, the clutch being replaced by a pedal which actually shifted

The Cotal transmission. On a 1936 Salmson S.4.D (*top left*), selection is via the tiny gate (*a*) under the steering wheel. On a Cotal, all the ratios can be used in either direction, which gave alarming possibilities to cars like the 3.5-litre Delahaye, capable of 110 mph (175 km/h). The engineer's drawing (*top right*) shows that the Cotal is an extension of the epicyclic system, in which planet wheels are spaced round a central sun wheel, meshing with it. Outside the planets, and meshing with them, is an annulus with teeth on its inner rim. On preselective boxes this annulus is held stationary by mechanically actuated band brakes, but on the Cotal, these latter are replaced by twin-plate clutches. The plates are held together by electro-magnets, and this eliminates the whole physical effort of shifting gear, without in any way affecting driver control. A switch was enough to shift the gear, though the conventional clutch pedal had still to be used when moving away from rest, and throttle actions when moving up and down were similar to those made with a sliding-type transmission

(*Centre*) The column-mounted selector of a preselective gearbox on a 1935 Armstrong Siddeley was labelled "low-medium-normal-high" rather than "1-2-3-4", a clear indication of how the factory thought the car should be driven. A safety stop was mounted on the quadrant between low and reverse, and the actual change was effected by depressing the gear-change pedal (which replaced the conventional clutch) after the gear had been selected. Electrical selection of gears was added in 1953. "It is possible," asserts the manual, "for the merest novice to drive in comfort and security, knowing that it is impossible to make a bad change of gear with its accompanying grinding noise, so distressing to the driver and passengers, to say nothing of the gearbox itself."

(*Bottom*) The workings of a simple synchromesh gearbox, with small cone clutches (*a*) interposed between sets of dogs (*b*). These cones make contact before the dogs begin to slide into mesh, the friction between the cones synchronizing the speed of the dogs. The drawings show the action on a downward shift from top to third. (*c*) Top. (*d*) Neutral. (*e*) Check. (*f*) Main shaft. (*g*) Third gear.

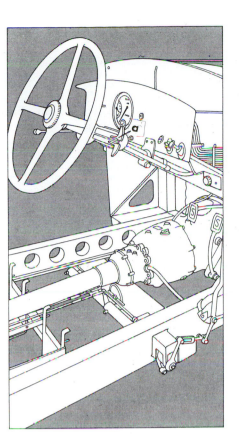

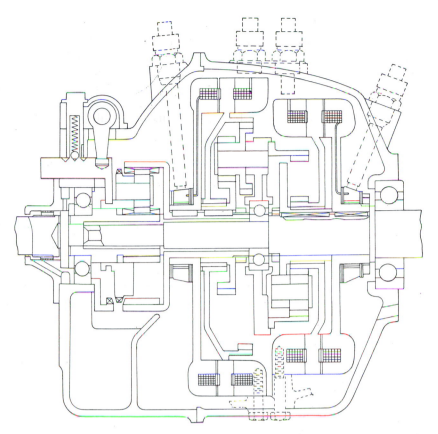

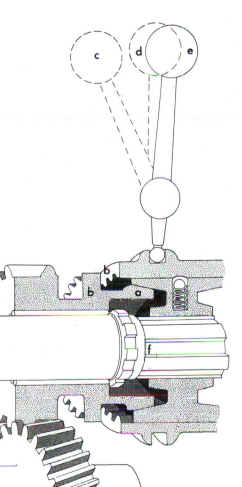

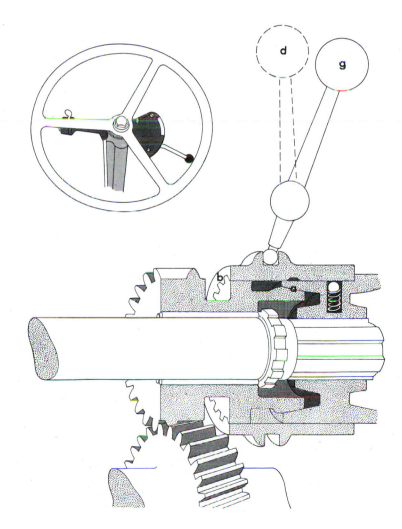

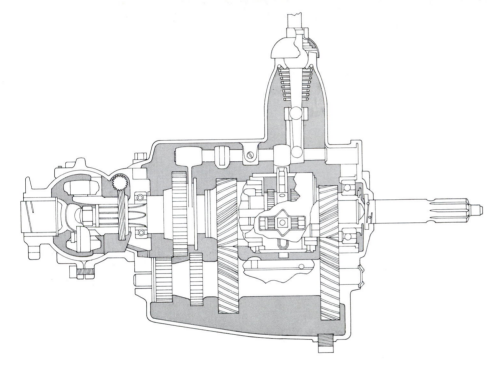

Cars and transmissions. (*Top left*) The 1932 60-series Buick convertible and (*top centre*) the 1935 50-series NA sedan of the same make, both overhead-valve straight-eights and both offering clash-proof, three-speed synchromesh transmissions. On the later example the radiator is becoming more of a grille, and one can detect the characteristic "sit" of the coil-spring independent front suspension adopted by Buick from 1934. The cross-section of a synchromesh transmission (*centre left*) forms an interesting contrast with the automatic on the opposite page, and illustrates the point that to make things simpler for the driver, one usually has to make them more complicated for the engineer and the maintenance man – even down to special transmission fluid for the automatic! Significantly, bottom gear was omitted from early synchromesh layouts, since few American drivers bothered with this ratio. In fact, the first mass-produced car to have an all-synchro arrangement was a most unlikely vehicle, the 1935 Hillman Minx (*bottom left*); it looks the uninspired family Ten it is, with a 30-hp 1.2-litre side-valve four-cylinder engine and indifferent cable-operated brakes. It was very flexible, and except in traffic or on hills, nothing much was gained from liberal use of the indirects – probably this is why Hillman decided to cut their costs and confine synchro to the top three gears after 1938. An intriguing halfway house (*centre right*) is the use of vacuum from the inlet manifold to give clutchless shifts, another novelty on 1932 Buicks. The selecting valve was actuated by the shifting bars of the transmission. Note, however, the retention of the clutch pedal: this was no case of belt-and-braces but was simply because the vacuum set-up functioned only between the two upper synchronized ratios. You did not get its assistance in low.

Painless shifting at last. The conservative 1935 17-hp Armstrong Siddeley (*right*), with custom cabrio-limousine coachwork by Salmons-Tickford, featured the Wilson preselective system. This still called for three pedals, the "clutch" actually shifting the gears already selected by a small quadrant on the steering-column. With a smallish engine and flywheel – the 17 ran to only 2.3 litres – physical effort was eliminated – and so were rude noises.

The 1940 Oldsmobile (*opposite, top right*) was the first car with two pedals and full automation: all one had to do was to select neutral, drive, or reverse, since the low range was strictly for emergencies like steep hills. The four base elements of the complex transmission (*below, main diagram*) were the fluid coupling with the flywheel (*a*), two planetary gear trains for the four forward ratios (*b, c*), and the reverse gear (*d*). The smaller picture shows the control system, located in the transmission sump. Actual power for the system was furnished by twin oil pumps at front and rear, the front unit providing immediate pressure starts, and the rear taking up its share once the car was in motion. Oil rather than spring pressure was used to actuate the majority of the elements, and a minor degree of manual control was exercised by the "kickdown", which ex-

erted extra force on the shifting valves when the accelerator was floored. It was, in fact, the only manual change-down viable in normal motoring, owing to the emergency nature of Low Range. Further, downshifts were impossible above 60 mph (100 km/h).

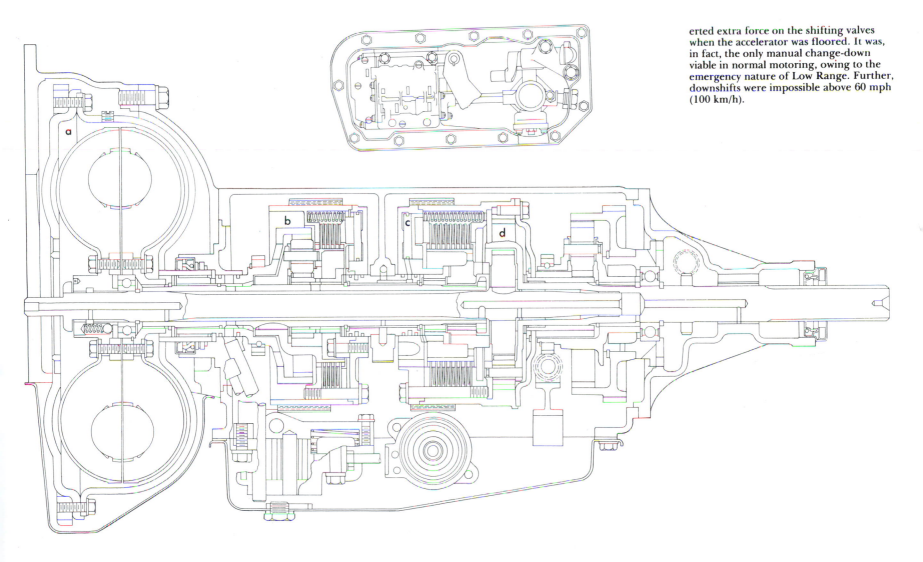

the gears after they had been preselected via a small lever on a column-mounted quadrant. (Some sports cars, notably MG and Lagonda, preferred a floor-mounted quadrant resembling today's "stick automatic"). Faults, complexity apart, were "clutch" slip, a plaintive syren-like wail, and a tendency, on big cars, for the flywheel to become argumentative if one forgot oneself and essayed an instant downshift. Daimler circumvented this last headache with their fluid flywheel, but preselection would become another casualty of the cost accountant, as the preselective gearbox was expensive both to make and to service. Fifteen British makers offered the system in 1934, but five years later, only Armstrong Siddeley, Daimler, and Lanchester remained loyal to "Wailing Wilson".

Wilson boxes were also tried by Isotta Fraschini in Italy and were standardized by some of the better French makers, notably Delahaye and Talbot, though the *système* Cotal was generally preferred on that side of the Channel, so much so that, by 1938, Delahaye were using up surplus Wilsons on less popular models. On this box the ratios were selected electromagnetically via a tiny column-mounted quadrant. Somewhat archaic was the use of a separate floor-mounted lever for forward and reverse, but the reward for unpredictable solenoids was the ability to utilize all four gears in either direction, which meant a theoretical 105 mph (170 km/h) maximum in reverse on a 3.5-litre Delahaye. This one, and Cord's rather similar electro-pneumatic shift of 1936, proved too delicate for the general public, though at least four British makers were experimenting with Cotals in 1939.

Now it was only one step forward to the true automatic. Georges Roesch of the English Talbot concern had already eliminated manual upward shifts (while maintaining a full manual override) on his 1934 version of the Wilson, and across the Atlantic Reo were offering a "self-shifter" in 1933. This was not a true automatic; it was, in effect, a two-speed dual-range box with automation confined within the individual ranges. Shifting from high to low range called for the use of the clutch; and, with only two forward speeds at the driver's immediate disposal, staying in high deprived the car of any noticeable acceleration. Much the same limitations applied to General Motors's first semi-automatic, offered on some 1938 Buicks and Oldsmobiles. The true torque converter, which required neither clutch nor an actual shift – beyond, of course, engagement of the emergency low range and of reverse – made its appearance on 1940 Oldsmobiles and was available on Cadillacs a year later. Its story properly belongs to the post-1945 era.

So, in effect, does that of column shift, magnified erroneously to the status of an automatic by American publicists. Its technical connotations are, in any case, peripheral, since the object was to clear the floor of obstructions and thus enable three people to share in comfort the bench seats of American cars. (In days when four doors were unnecessary, of course, the shift lever had been mounted on the right-hand side, still a U-feature on British cars until the general acceptance of automatic.) The best that could be said of the new arrangement was that it was superior to the strange dashboard linkages that accompanied the prentice years of front-wheel drive. Some of these assortments of cables are best not inspected, though they worked better than one might imagine.

By the mid-thirties, front-wheel drive, though a breach of the Panhard shibboleths, was no longer regarded as rank heresy. Though rear-wheel drive remained in the majority – in 1939, neither the United States nor Italy offered anything else – *traction avant* had been proven in use. In Germany, from 1931 on, DKW led the field; they had been joined by Adler a year later. Nor were these rare luxury items; the combined output of the two factories ran to around sixty thousand units in 1937 alone. Czechoslovakia's smaller, DKW-inspired two-stroke automobiles all used it, and since 1934, there had been an even more

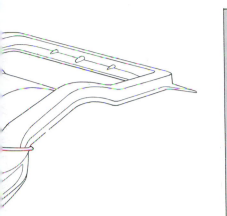

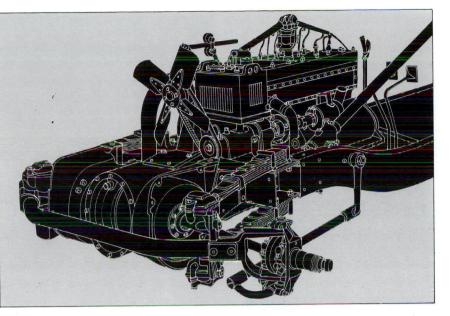

(*Far left*) The ingredients of the unitary body fitted to the 1939 Opel Kapitän. Here the pressed-steel floor unit incorporates what would normally be the chassis frame.

It is easy to see why the stylists went for the long, low look. They had to, when, as on the 1929 Cord, the entire drive unit was mounted ahead of 4.9 litres of straight-eight, seen here in side view (*below*). Of 205 inches (5.2 m) of automobile, 46 inches (1.2 m) were hood. The motor had to be turned round so that it would rotate anticlockwise, while the front brakes were inboard, and gearbox, clutch, and differential were all mounted in unit. The curious linkage running across the top of the motor, seen in the three-quarters view (*left*), past the high-tension leads, connects the gearbox to the dash-mounted gearshift, an arrangement also found on Adlers and Amilcar Compounds.

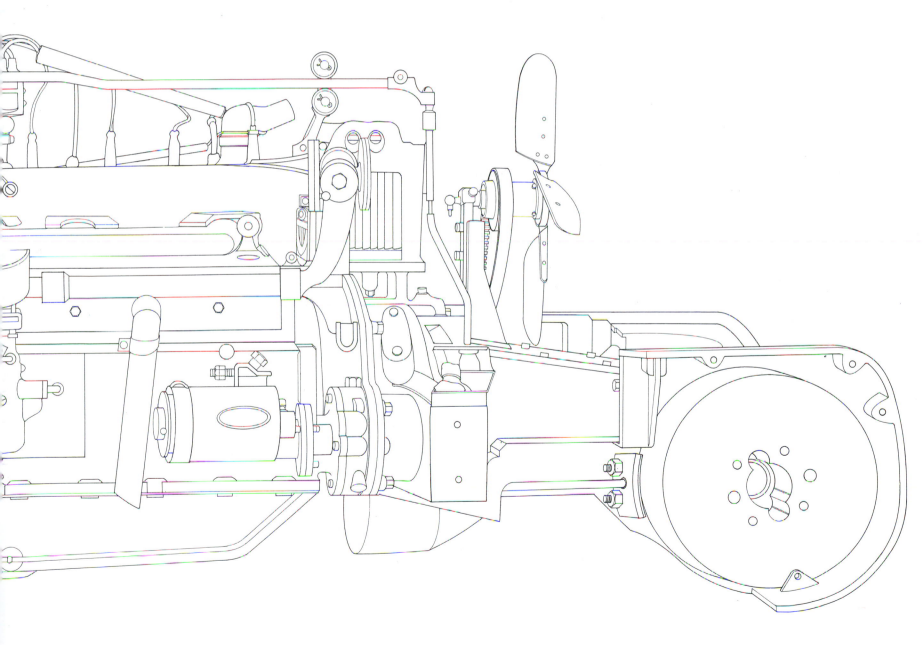

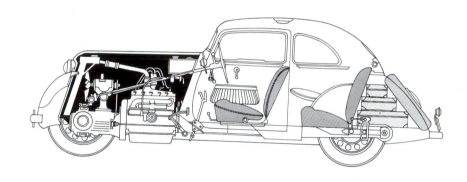

Front-wheel drive and rear engines. The 1934 Mercedes-Benz 130 H (*top left*) shows its formidable overhang from the rear, which made it something of a nightmare in crosswinds. A logical and far more manageable descendant is the Volkswagen (*opposite, top*), here seen in 1947 form, still without synchromesh or hydraulic brakes, but now with the definitive 1,131-cc 25-hp motor in place of 1939's 985-cc unit. This is one of the first cars to reach England, where the importers two-toned it to relieve the austerity of Wolfsburg's drab monochromes. DKW (*top right*), Adler (*centre*), and BSA (*bottom left*) all favoured front-wheel drive in the 1930s. The Adler cutaway drawing (*centre right*) highlights the extravagance of putting the gearbox out front, even if it does make for a length of hood more suggestive of three litres than the car's actual 995 cc. No wonder the artist made great play with the trunk space available! More frugal in this respect was the DKW (this is a 1939 model) on which the 684-cc two-cycle water-cooled twin engine was mounted transversely at the front of a simple backbone, but the chance to anticipate Alec Issigonis's Mini was frustrated by the make-image. The parent Auto Union firm liked their cheap baby car to resemble a scaled-down Horch, and this coach-built *luxus* cabriolet (lesser models had fabric bodies) made an excellent job of it. It was, alas, expensive, overweight, and under-powered, being little more than the German equivalent of a Sunbeam-Talbot Ten. The BSA, Britain's sole volume-production *traction* in pre-war days, had a ten-year run in three- and four-wheeled forms, always with independent suspension by eight transverse springs (four each side) and with inboard front brakes. Ingenious it certainly was, but opinions were divided on its handling, and the 1,075-cc side-valve four-cylinder engine fitted to this Scout kept top speed down to a laboured 60 mph (95–100 km/h).

(*Centre left*) With heavy cars, some means

was needed to reduce braking effort without any loss of efficiency. Much favoured in the twenties and still used on European cars in the thirties was the Dewandre system, making use of inlet manifold suction. Release of the accelerator pedal causes manifold pressure to drop, and by connecting the manifold to a servo cylinder, it was possible to put this to work. The servo cylinder is exhausted of air, and atmospheric pressure drives a piston inwards, thus exerting force upon the braking system. Hispano-Suiza and Rolls-Royce used a different type of servo in the form of a friction clutch mounted on the side of the gearbox and rotated by the transmission.

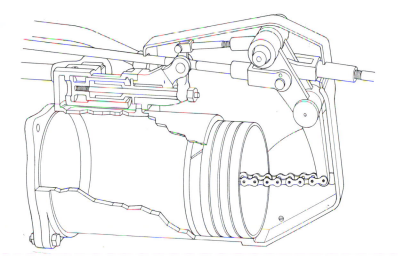

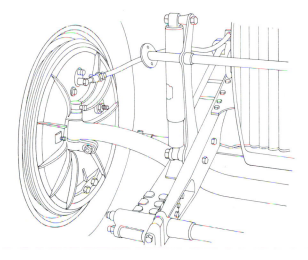

The ultimate for the grand tourist in the thirties was Bugatti's Type 57 (*left*), first seen at the 1933 Shows. After the franc slid three years later, it became a bargain at less than £1,000 ($5,000) in England. The lines of this regular, early-model *coach Ventoux* are spoilt by the exaggerated rake of the windshield, but the twin-cam straight-eight engine was tractable, and 95 mph (150–155 km/h) presented no problems. Bugatti had no truck with detachable cylinder heads, synchromesh, or independent suspension, but though early 57s retained mechanical brakes, hydraulic actuation (*centre right*) had been adopted by 1938. Note the generously ribbed drums and also the hydraulic piston-type dampers adopted at the same time. These replaced the complicated De Ram friction type, said to cost around £150 ($750) a set and to need "works" tuning. The Bugatti's 3,257-cc engine gave 135 hp, or 160 with the optional supercharger (Type 57C). In 1939, a stock 57C sedan put 112 miles (179 km) into a *standing-start* hour at Montlhéry Autodrome. The only real snag about such motoring in the grand manner was that there wasn't a friendly Bugatti dealer in every town, even in France, and the machinery was beyond the ministrations of the average mechanic.

important contender – Citroën, France's number one seller. The principle of "pull instead of push" made for vastly superior road-holding. Further, the absence of a drive shaft running the length of the car made not only for greater legroom, but also for a lower centre of gravity. What it did not yet achieve was the compactness associated with latter-day expositions of the formula of "putting all the works up one end". True, the DKW's vertical, twin two-stroke engine was transversely disposed, but nobody had devised any other means of fitting in anything bigger. Even when DKW themselves began tests of a three-cylinder engine in 1939, they had recourse to the longitudinal mounting still in general use. Add to this space-consuming arrangement a gearbox in front of the power unit, and the result was apt to be abnormal length, capitalized on the original straight-eight Cord of 1929 by some brilliant and much-imitated front-end styling. The practical disadvantages were heavier steering at low speeds, a poor lock (Citroën's 15/6 of 1939 required a 46-foot, or a 14-metre, turning circle), greater vulnerability in head-on collisions, and complicated gear linkages. A dashboard location was generally favoured, though the Alvis and early BSAs retained the old right-hand floor shift.

Where front-wheel drive was backed by adequate finances (as already mentioned, Citroën had to be rescued by Michelin) and a good service network, it succeeded. By the outbreak of the Second World War, Citroën's potential was some fifty thousand units a year, DKW's forty-five thousand, and Adler's perhaps twenty-five thousand. That such heresy was not for the small maker was demonstrated when Rosengart of France attempted to build – or, more strictly, assemble and trim – Adlers for the local market. The venture lasted less than eighteen months, after which the Parisian firm reverted to its original theme – gallicized editions of the Austin Seven. (They would later contrive an attractive sports sedan by fitting 11CV Citroën mechanical elements into their own platform frames and bodies.) Large front-wheel drive cars were beset with problems of weight transference. In the United States, E.L. Cord had two skirmishes with the system: the first, the L29, succumbed to the aforementioned weight-transference weakness, as well as to the problems caused by the Depression; the second, the better-engineered 810 of 1936, was altogether too complicated for Americans accustomed to a diet of the painless and insipid, not to mention flat-rate servicing and factory exchange units!

Rear engines played little part in the 1930s, for all the attractions of that perfect aerodynamic shape that was the prime chimera of 1934. One of John Tjaarda's styling prototypes for the Lincoln-Zephyr featured an engine at the back, but, though it reached the test stage, the end-product reverted to the *système* Panhard. Once again, linkages were a headache; a worse one was directional instability in crosswinds, which showed up only too well on Europe's new motorways. The big air-cooled Tatra V8, though quiet at speed and astonishingly efficient – 100 mph (160 km/h) on three-litres-odd and less than 80 bhp – was addicted to sudden and vicious rear-end breakaway. So was the little 130H Mercedes-Benz with its formidably overhung tail, though this underpowered creature disliked anything more than 50–55 mph (85 km/h). There was also the problem of combining a rear-mounted engine with rearward visibility, a commodity lacking not only on the Tatra, but also on Ferdinand Porsche's definitive Volkswagen, visible if not on sale by the latter half of 1938. The Volkswagen did, however, represent an intelligent approach to mass transportation in a sophisticated age and summarized much of the period's technical thinking. The recipe embraced a lightly stressed, frost-proof, air-cooled, flat-four engine of short-stroke type, capable of holding its appointed 3,200 rpm all day, allied to an aerodynamic shape offering the minimum of wind resistance. Here was the shape of things to come, and in more senses than

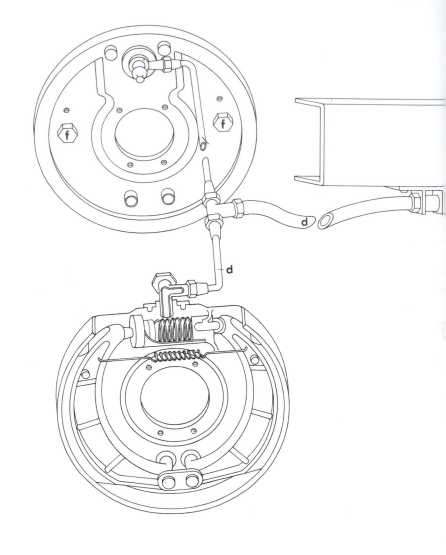

Popular on British cars – Austin, Daimler, Rover, and SS were among its users – was the Girling rod-operated system, on which almost the entire operating mechanism (*bottom*) is in tension, thus obviating one of the worst snags of cables. The brake shoes (*a*) are expanded by a cone (*b*).

On hydraulic brakes (*top*), pipe lines and pistons replace the rods or cables and levers of earlier brake systems. Depression of the pedal (*a*) displaces fluid in a master cylinder (*b*), through the movement of a

piston (*c*). Pipes (*d*) connect the master cylinder to working cylinders (*e*), one in each wheel, and the fluid displaced from the master cylinder exerts pressure on opposed pistons in the working cylinder. Uniformity of pressure in an enclosed system gives perfect compensation. Though general practice in the United States by 1939, the system did not finally take over from mechanical arrangements until the end of our period. (*f*) Shoe adjusters. (*g*) To front brakes. (*h*) Supply tank.

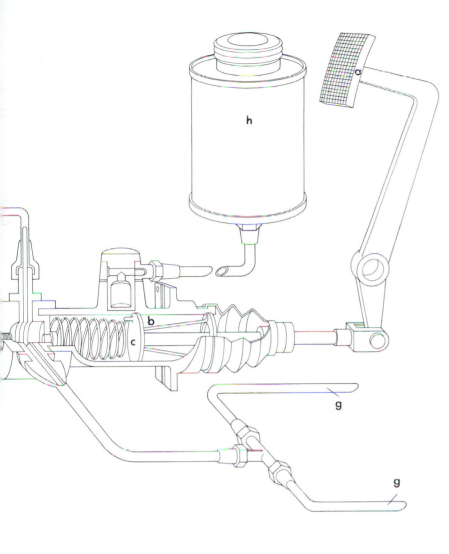

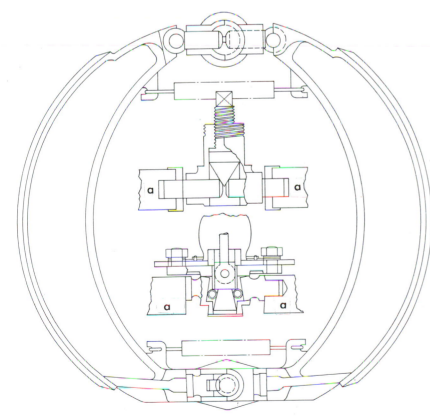

mere volume production. The Beetle's forty-year span would beat the Model T Ford by a substantial margin, even if total sales probably outran the Ford's by a mere eight or nine per cent.

In the braking department, of course, the Volkswagen was inadequate even by 1938's standards. The Third Reich housed the sternest of cost accountants; the car had, in theory, to be sold for RM990 (about £56, or $280!), and thus, the Beetle's anchors were old-fashioned cable-actuated mechanicals. They would continue to be just that for another twelve years.

Retardation had made considerable strides in the 1930s, albeit the picture is mainly one of a consolidation of ideas evolved in the previous decade. A better-class European or American sedan of the middle or later 1930s should cause no one any anxiety in the road conditions of half a century later, provided it be driven at the speeds for which it was designed – a steady 60 mph (100 km/h) in the case of bigger models, or 45–50 mph (75–80 km/h) in the under 1,500-cc class. It is only when one samples the period's *grandes routières* – such as the legendary V12 Lagonda – that one recognizes that even dual-circuit hydraulics working in adequately-cooled drums of generous diameter are not suited for 100 mph (160 km/h) on modern highways.

Brake cooling would, however, be a problem of the future. Spoked wheels of one kind and another would be regular equipment – apart from a preference in Continental Europe for the full disc – right up to 1937.

By the beginning of our period, the internal-expanding brake had won through; the earlier contracting type with its exposed and dirt-prone bands had been one of the casualties of 1929. Also a casualty was, thank goodness, the transmission brake. Long banished to the hand-operated emergency circuit, it had but two major adherents by 1935, Fiat and Chrysler. It was a snare to the unskilled, who sometimes forgot that its only safe function was parking and that habitual use at speeds above walking pace could have interesting effects on the drive line.

Mechanical systems saw the decade through, mainly because not everyone trusted fragile rubber pipes and potentially corrosive fluids, and because plastic was in its infancy. By 1939, however, hydraulics were virtually universal in the United States, while important European users were Morris, Vauxhall, and Rootes in Britain; Mercedes-Benz, BMW, Hansa, and Opel in Germany; Volvo in Sweden; Fiat and Lancia in Italy; and Citroën, though not Peugeot or Renault, in France.

Of the alternatives, cables had the merits of simplicity, cheapness, and of being a convenient means of linking the hand-brake to all four wheels. (This linkage was a regular concomitant of the much-used Bendix system.) Among the disadvantages was a tendency for the cables to stretch, giving crabwise stops unless they were frequently adjusted. Rod-operated types like the Girling, though less temperamental, called for heavy pedal pressure. Nonetheless, the hydraulic brake's even and progressive retardation won through. Servo systems, usually of vacuum type, were becoming popular at the end of the 1920s, when Hillman and Citroën had been among their devotees. In the depressed 1930s, they were reserved for large, vast, and expensive models such as the great American classics. Hispano-Suiza's gearbox servo was used by that company and by Rolls-Royce, though one of the defects of such assistance was a tendency to require a few seconds' thinking time when every second counted. Another common disease of the 1920s, a "loss of interest" below 15 mph, was, however, seldom encountered in later years.

As yet, power steering lay in the future, and few designers had adopted the precise rack-and-pinion gear almost universal today, albeit it was found on all front-wheel-drive Adlers, and on parallel Citroëns from 1936 onwards. The main concern of manufacturers, especially in

Car of the Decade: if there'd been international panels voting on such subjects in the 1930s, Citroën's *traction* must surely have taken the title. The skeleton view stands for the main structure as found on some three-quarter òf a million four- and six-cylinder machines turned out between 1934 and 1957. Clearly visible are the main structural members and the front horns on which the power pack was mounted. Notice that though the shape has been tidied up (there are, for instance, no running boards), it reveals no exaggerated "streamline" tendencies of the type rampant at the time. Headroom is adequate and takes full advantage of the flat floor, the hood is side-opening, and the engine (if not the electrics or transmission) is more accessible than on many of the Citroën's later competitors. The dashboard (*top centre*) is typically austere, with the familiar single dial incorporating fuel and oil gaugès, ammeter, speedometer, and odometer. Note the traditional

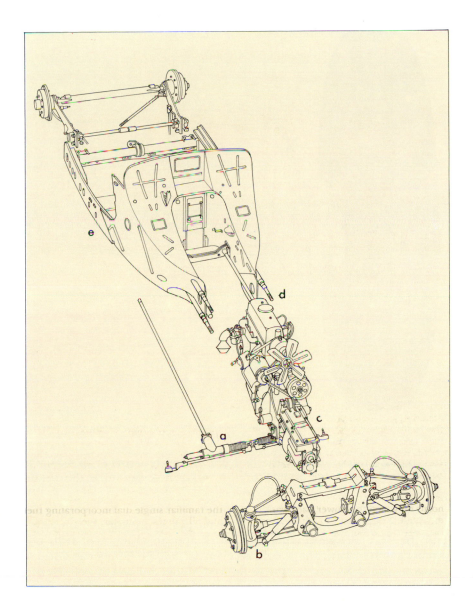

Citroën

opening windshield, though there are two discordant notes for 1934 – the pistol-grip handbrake under the dash, and the dashboard gear shift for the three-speed synchromesh transmission. Its action was very awkward, though BSA, DKW, and Adler used similar levers; the Adler's was, however, direct-coupled to the box and easier to handle.

(*Top right*) Citroën *traction* exploded and bared of body panels, showing the rack and pinion steering (*a*) adopted during 1936, the ingenious torsion-bar front suspension (*b*) which kept the front wheels permanently vertical and parallel, the engine-gearbox unit (*c*) and its mounting horns (*d*), and the base structure (*e*) com-

prising firewall and flat floor pressing. At the rear there is a simple tubular dead axle (*f*) with transverse torsion bar springing (*g*). Much was made of the wheel-out power pack, but Citroën maintenance was never that easy! The front and rear views show one of the first 15/6s of 1939 but reveal neither its impressive length of nearly 16 ft (4.9 m), which made for a turning circle of 46 ft (14 m). Definitely not a car for shopping in crowded city streets! Note the outward-opening trunk, an improvement on the first *tractions*, on which only the spare wheel was accessible without first shifting the rear seat.

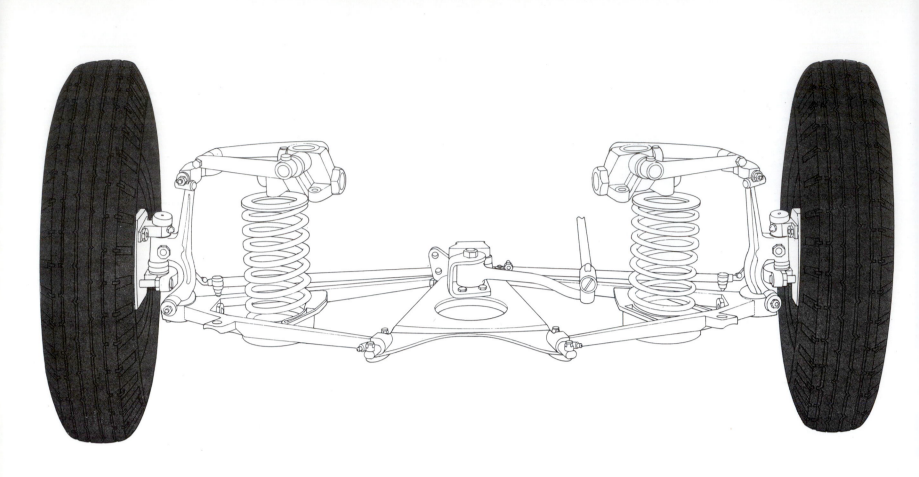

the United States, was not the best line through a corner, but how to reconcile the growing weight of the modern sedan with the faster-growing proportion of women drivers.

Hitherto, this had not been a major problem. The fair sex had preferred smaller cars, European favourites being the Austin Seven and the 5CV Peugeot. Open bodywork and an absence of frills and gimmickry had kept the weight of even a 1,500-cc family car down to one ton, and this went for the well-loved Model A Ford as well. Hence, two-and-a-half turns from lock to lock were viable without straining Madame's muscles. Manoeuvring some 1.8 tons of straight-eight Buick into a car park was, however, something quite different, and the only way out was a lower ratio: four-and-a-half or maybe five turns. Between 1932 and 1939, the Ford V8's steering ratio fell progressively year by year; while the original Model-18 had been "quick" on the hands, by the end of our period, keen rallyistes attached traction-engine-style handles to the steering wheels, the better to wind their cars through the wiggle-woggles of the Monte Carlo and similar events.

Perhaps the greatest advances – or at least the groundwork for them – came in the realm of suspension. Not that everyone agreed: more than one factory tried independent front springing, only to abandon it, in Rover's case too late for its deletion from the catalogue's first edition! As late as 1939, a leaf spring at each corner did the job for British mass-produced cars, with the exception of some Standards and the American-inspired Vauxhalls. Renault combined semi-elliptics at the front with a Ford-like transverse spring at the rear, while Ford themselves retained the bouncy, all-transverse arrangements that had been their hallmark for a good thirty years. Renault was, however, almost the sole conservative left in France, while in Germany, everything had gone over to the new order, with the exception of those cars built at Ford's Cologne factory and of a few older, luxury-car types. Italy's solitary cart-sprung contribution was the Bianchi, by now in token production only.

Thus the way of the world at the end of our period. In 1930, there

were few heretics, of whom Lancia and Röhr were the most important. Shock absorbers were, however, universal, with hydraulic types replacing the primitive friction arrangements of earlier days. On luxury models (Rolls-Royce and Packard) they could be set to adjust the ride while the car was in motion.

Independent front suspension was, of course, motivated by different reasons on opposite sides of the Atlantic, as comparative drives in (say) a Lancia and a Buick will quickly reveal. In the United States, the objective was the so-called "boulevard ride", calculated to damp out the shocks to be expected on the poor surfaces of the backwoods, both at home and in such vital export markets as Argentina, Australia, and South Africa. General Motors's notorious "knee action" was publicized by photographs showing cars with conventional and modern suspensions each with one front wheel resting on a wood block some 6 in (15 cm) high. It was firmly pointed out that the "one with the knees" was the one also retaining a horizontal roof-line. This was true: bumps were smoothed out with commendable regularity. What the customer was left to discover for himself was that the cars rolled and pitched most disconcertingly in corners, while sudden braking caused the "knees" to curtsey frantically. (A switch to torsion bars on some later General Motors models was said to counteract this party piece, but it merely reversed it. The nose went up first!) Later coil-and-wishbone systems of the short-and-long-arm persuasion were much better, but Americans remained unconvinced. Chevrolet themselves would retain a beam-axle option in their catalogues right up to 1940.

Not that European designers were unconcerned with poor surfaces. The protagonists of sophisticated suspensions were Czechoslovakia and Germany – the former still with notoriously rough roads, and the latter desperately in need of foreign exchange. Germany's best export markets were Central and Eastern Europe, Scandinavia, and South Africa, all of them unkind to cars. European designers had also, however, a keen interest in handling, and the best torsion-bar systems, notably those of BMW and Citroën, were as sure-footed in the rough as in the

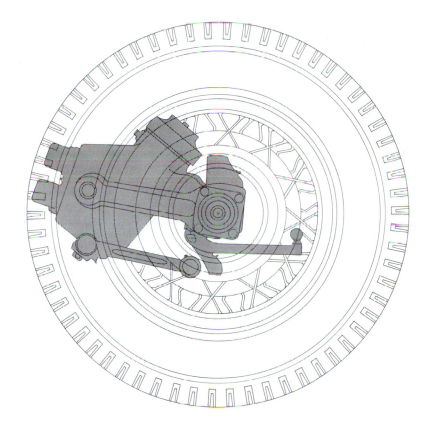

Suspension layouts. The short-and-long-arm coil system, here seen (*far left*) on a 1934 Oldsmobile, was effectively the prototype for later coil arrangements, whereas the Dubonnet "knees" (*left*) carried the front wheel on a single arm extending forward from the king pin. Hydraulic shock absorbers were incorporated into the system, which was oil-filled and, therefore, theoretically self-lubricating. Levels had, however, to be topped up at 25,000-mile (40,000 km) intervals, and owners did not always bother, so that heavy wear added to the Dubonnet's disconcerting habit of "curtseying" under hard braking. American ideas of suspension are, however, reflected in Vauxhall's 1935 publicity. Of the two sedans—the one in the upper centre a 1934 with semi-elliptics at the front—it was the car with knees that maintained the even roof-line. The Evenkeel independent front wheel suspension (*bottom*) on the 1936–47 Hillmans and Humbers was based on an equivalent construction on the 1935 Studebaker. Its characteristic was that the lateral springs doubled as the lower stub axle. The shock-absorber was mounted on the frame and was actuated by the upper stub axle via a linking rod. A shaped rubber cushion on the upper stub axle coped with excessive bumps.

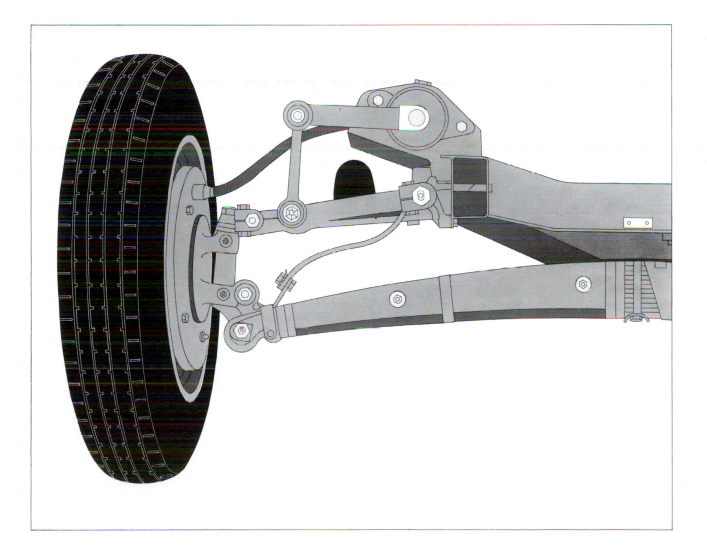

When one considers that it appeared in 1922, it's astonishing that the Austin Seven – 1930 (*top*) and 1935 (*opposite, top right*) – was still in production as late as the spring of 1939. More remarkably, its sales increased in the 1930s, peaking in 1935 (27,280 units). Main differences over a five-year period were coupled brakes and an extra forward gear, though this was added at the wrong end, giving an underdrive for assaults on the vertical. Weight went up faster than anything else – from 1,080 lb (490 kg) to 1,358 (615 kg), an increment which gave the more modern babies of Ford and Morris an even greater advantage.

In the 1,100-cc class, two late thirties offerings were the German Hansa of 1937 (*bottom*) and the 1938 Peugeot 202 from France (*opposite, centre right*). With its beetling hood and headlamps tucked away behind the grille (the battery lived there as well!), the Peugeot looks the more modern design. Its 30-hp overhead-valve four-cylinder engine had the near-square dimensions of 68×78 mm, and front wheels were independently sprung, but a three-speed transmission was deemed sufficient, and on pre-war versions brakes were mechanical. It was, however, an admirable workhorse and tided its makers over into 1949 and the advent of the unitary 203. Some 104,000 were made, as against perhaps 20,000 Hansas between 1934 and the war – but then Carl Borgward's empire was still young. This Hansa featured a typically German backbone frame with transverse-leaf independent front suspension and a swing-axle rear end, while brakes were hydraulic from the start; so were four forward speeds. It was as modestly rated (27.5 hp from 1,088 cc) as the Peugeot, but better looking. Oddly, the Hansa 1100 was scheduled for elimination under the Schell plan for rationalizing the German automobile industry, but its good export sales earned it a reprieve, and the model was still listed in Sweden in 1940.

Teutonic half-measures. By 1939, the six-cylinder Type 320 Mercedes-Benz cabriolet (*opposite, left*) had all-independent springing – indeed, its predecessors had been so endowed for six years – but the chassis was otherwise conventional and the engine a stolid and lethargic flat-head. Eight years its senior is the Austro-Daimler Alpine Eight (*bottom*) from over the border in Vienna. The Austrian car is also of greater technical interest. True, the front axle rides on longitudinal half-elliptic springs, but clearly visible is the swing-axle rear end, tailor-made for twisty roads and poor surfaces, if sometimes a handful in the wet. The frame is a tubular backbone with outriggers for the body, fourth gear is an overdrive for fast cruising, and both cylinder block and barrels are of light alloy. Alas, all this weight-paring was exploited by Austrian coach-builders, and most Alpine Eights weighed well over two tons, and sometimes nearly three. The engine's 115 hp weren't really enough, but then Österreichisches Daimler weren't after the sports-car market. If performance was what you wanted, you opted for the six-cylinder Bergmeister – a litre less of engine, more compact dimensions, and five extra hp.

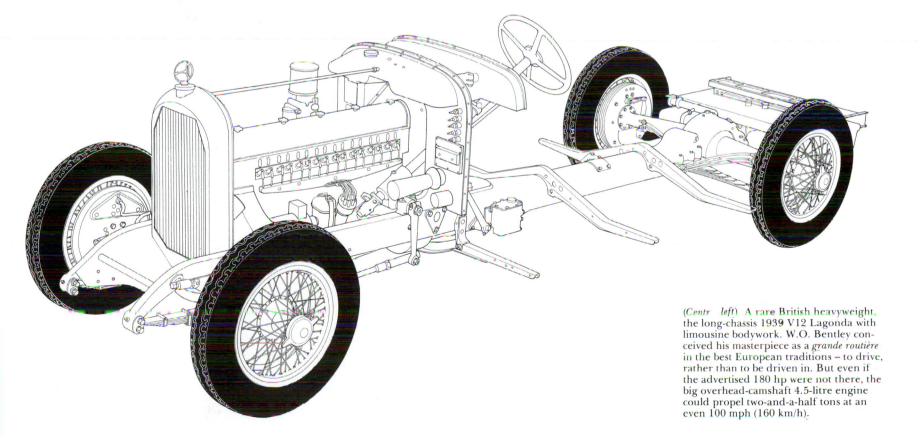

(*Centr   left*) A rare British heavyweight, the long-chassis 1939 V12 Lagonda with limousine bodywork. W.O. Bentley conceived his masterpiece as a *grande routière* in the best European traditions – to drive, rather than to be driven in. But even if the advertised 180 hp were not there, the big overhead-camshaft 4.5-litre engine could propel two-and-a-half tons at an even 100 mph (160 km/h).

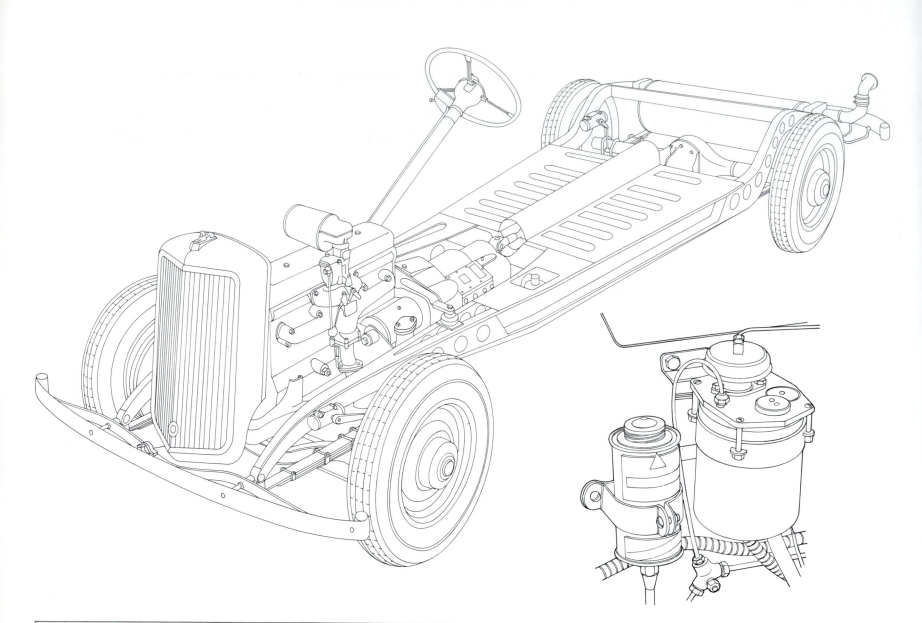

First steps to unitary construction. The 1939 16-hp Armstrong Siddeley (*above*) had a separate chassis, conventional suspension, and mechanical brakes, as well as the preselective gearbox standardized on the make since 1932. The "sealed floor fume-proof frame" was, however, rather more than that, since it gave the extra rigidity of a further box section, to which the body was bolted. Officially, it was the first Armstrong Siddeley not supplied as a chassis to special coachbuilders, and some cheapening is apparent in the stylizing of the sphinx mascot. Intended as a 70-mph (112 km/h) five-passenger sedan for "volume" production, it accounted for only some 950 units before war intervened.

The bare bones of an early unitary structure (*left*), the 1,196-cc Lancia Augusta of 1933, are interesting as they reveal great structural strength. Also interesting is another space and weight-saving device favoured by European small-car makers (among them, Triumph), the pillarless four-door configuration. It made for easy entry and exit but rattled fearsomely in old age, causing the doors to twist and lose their fit. Draughts were also a problem.

Built-in amenities. The Bijur system of automatic chassis lubrication (*above right*), here seen on a 1934 Rover, had reached Europe from the United States in the early 1930s. The reservoir was easily accessible, and the system was operated by that useful standby, inlet manifold depression. An elaborate system of metering jets was used, the grease gun being reserved for awkward places like the splines of the propeller shaft and the rear wheel hubs. Alas! tiny pipes became clogged with old age, and the cars of the 1930s had a long, enforced innings in front of them. Often the automatics were dispensed with in old age.

smooth. Lancia's coils and sliding pillars had proved their worth since 1922, while also excellent was Fiat's conventional coil-spring set up on the first 1100s, though this one was abnormally sensitive to tyre pressures. A significant factor of the better European designs was that they retained a wheel at each corner, thus attaining a superior weight distribution. Outside the realm of the big mock-Americans, one seldom encountered the monumental degree of overhang common to Detroit's efforts.

The all-independent system was largely confined to Germany, Austria, and Czechoslovakia; elsewhere conservatism and the cost accountant conspired to exclude it. It was not a system that could be grafted on to an existing chassis design. Even the pioneering Austro-Daimlers of the late 1920s, which combined independent rear springing with a beam front axle, used Karl Rabe's new tubular backbone frames (first pioneered by the Czech Ledvinka). Further, the then fashionable swing-axle arrangement had its limitations. Longitudinal corrugations often caught it unawares, and while it was admirably suited to cope with the stolid side-valve engines of the contemporary touring Mercedes-Benz, it could assume frightening attitudes when asked to transmit the 180 bhp of a supercharged straight-eight with blower engaged. Significantly, independent rear suspension promised to become one of the casualties of the inflationary 1970s.

Tubular backbone frames might have been the concomitants of Germany's new suspension units, but the conventional ladder-type chassis had plenty of life left in it. Design philosophy had, admittedly, changed from the whippy and inadequately braced structures of the 1920s, while one constructional feature hardly ever seen after 1930 was the use of a separate U-section sub-frame for engine and gearbox. Amidships cruciform bracing was perhaps the most important technical legacy of the first Cord, 1929's L29, and though there were still some horrors about (the Hornet and Scorpion were by no means the sole cases of haphazard up-engining in the Depression years), cruciforms of one kind and another had become accepted practice by 1935, assisted by rigid box-section side-members of generous depth. On bigger cars it was not uncommon to add further supplementary K-bracing aft of the gearbox, though the switch towards unit construction of motor and transmission tended to make this superfluous. The old disease of chassis flexing – which broke fuel pipes and helped bodies to disintegrate – was almost a thing of the past, except where the frame came out overweight and its side-members were too liberally drilled. Morris Eights of the 1935–38 period were notable offenders in this direction.

Curiously centralized "one-shot" systems of chassis lubrication, found on many a middle-class or luxury model of the 1930s, were not destined to survive long into the post-war years. Pressing a pedal on the floor every hundred miles or so might be a great deal more painless than a messy session with the grease gun (and cheaper than paying someone else to do it), but to be successful, pain-killers had to be foolproof as well as therapeutic, and one-shot systems were not. Hence, along with built-in jackets and self-adjusting tappets, they vanished from the scene, aided and abetted by horrible memories of "gummed up" vehicles retrieved from six years of storage in 1945! The Jackalls beloved of British makers could be restored to health with a medicinal dose of mineral oil, but the top end of a twelve-cylinder Rolls-Royce motor required more drastic remedies. Hence, the grease gun returned to favour, until such time as the industry came up with components "lubricated for life".

Unitary construction of chassis and body posed a large question mark throughout the latter half of the decade. The integration of the automobile was primarily the work of the stylists, who had intruded upon the American scene in the later 1920s. Indeed, their endeavours were all too often at variance with those of the engineers, especially in realms such as underhood accessibility (an alligator hood streamlines better, but the sides won't come off so that you can get at the fuel pump) and facia design (stylized instruments are all too often illegible). Nevertheless, however a car might look – and models like the Sixty Special Cadillac of 1938 contained no detectable appendages or afterthoughts – it was still essentially a chassis and running gear designed by engineers and wedded to a body created by artists. Even if the custom-coachwork industry had gone into a steady decline, many traditional chassis manufacturers (Rolls-Royce, Maybach, and Alvis, for instance) made no bodies themselves, and their measure of control over what went onto their chassis was limited to a right to withhold the warranty if the coachwork exceeded a statutory weight.

At less exalted levels, of course, a manufacturer had to budget for bodies as well as mechanical elements, and here the unitary system had its attractions. Foremost of these was structural strength: Chrysler and Citroën dropped cars off cliffs to demonstrate the advantages of the new idiom, and Morris staged a series of radio-controlled crashes to prove that 1939's integral Ten sedan was stronger than the separate-chassis type listed in 1938. On the debit side, a switch to unitary methods involved fearsome tooling bills, the amortization of which called for a long production run.

Worse still, the unitary system was inflexible: sedans and station wagons (the latter, as we shall see, as yet hardly a part of the motoring scene) represented the limit of stylistic diversity. When Vauxhall's Australian clients wanted a tourer on their new H-series Ten, a separate-chassis variant had to be offered, and Lancia made a practice of such a type to keep the specialist coachbuilders happy. Even more important were the economic limitations imposed on interim improvements. One could extract a few more brake horses from the engine by adding an extra carburettor. One could change the grille, lengthen the boot slightly, or maybe even alter the shape of the front fenders, provided that these latter remained separate entities, as they did on the original Citroën *traction*. Anything else – even suspension alterations on a major scale – would upset the even tenor of the road to amortization.

The owner had his worries, too. While he was more likely to survive a major crash, his car might suffer sufficient distortion in a minor one to make it an insurance write-off. Further more, body rust, already a problem with cheap pressed-steel coachwork, now meant structural rust as well.

The United States was logically the one country that could afford unitary methods. It was also the one that needed them not! Americans still demanded a choice of six or seven bodies per model, and going unitary spelt goodbye to convertibles. In any case, the same sheet metal was expected to last two or three years, and if a model failed to sell forty thousand a year during that period, it was no longer economically viable, chassis or no chassis. This, however, did not stop General Motors from trying out the new techniques, first on Opels in Germany, and then at the British Vauxhall factory. By 1940, all their European models had dispensed with a separate chassis, even if the home team would not take the plunge until 1959.

Semi-unitary methods were less expensive: once the car was put together, chassis and body were inseparable, but the two elements were constructed separately and then welded or bolted up. Typical of this technique were the Chrysler Airflow (1934) and the Lincoln Zephyr (1936). The Chrysler was, in fact, an interesting anticipation of the space-frame techniques which would emerge on specialist Italian sports cars in the late 1940s. The body was a "cage" to which the panels were welded. In Britain Austin typified a different and more gradual approach to the unitary ideal: on the company's last pre-war Eights and

Unitary structures. The Vauxhall (*bottom*) of 1938 is almost the copybook configuration and immensely strong. A heavy cross member is needed at the rear with rear-wheel drive, while additional strength was achieved by ribs on the underside, which also helped to cut out drumming. This drawing serves to explain the catastrophic effect of corrosion, especially in floor or wheel arches, but with long enough runs the system paid off. Vauxhall's H-type shape sat it out for ten years from 1938, and the L-type (1948–51) wasn't all that different. With front-wheel drive, of course, one doesn't need half as much bracing at the rear, and J.A. Grégoire's Amilcar-Compound (*opposite, top*), a sensation of the 1937 Shows, used light alloys to keep weight down still further. The short side members incorporated the sills and were tied at the front by a simple cross-member, while also part of the structure was the firewall, incorporated on this one with the windshield pillars. Alas! it was a case of too little, too late – less than seven hundred had been delivered before the Fall of France.

Unitaries clothed. Britain's 1939 Morris Ten (*top*), the 1300 Hanomag from Germany (*opposite, bottom left*), and the

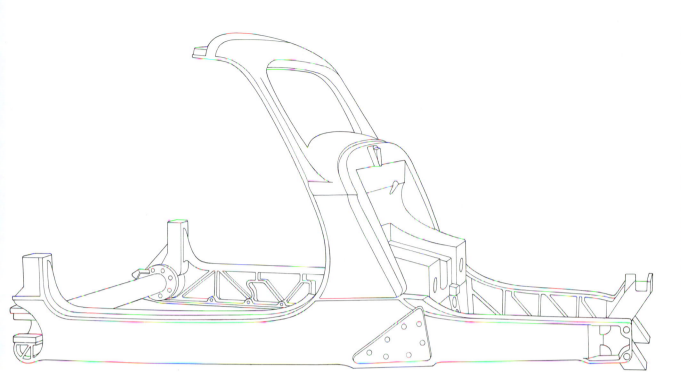

Nash 600 introduced in 1941 (*bottom right*) have conventional drive-lines, while on the 1938 Amilcar Compound (*centre left*) the drive is taken to the front wheels. For all its low build and absence of running boards, the Amilcar's looks are spoilt by the usual mock-American grille, while there's nothing in the appearance of the Morris or the Nash to suggest unorthodox methods of construction. The Hanomag's teardrop shape owes much to the high cruising speeds possible on Germany's new *Autobahnen*, though. The Nash is, by the way, the final 1948 manifestation of the original 60 series, though only the grille differs in substance from the first cars.

Odd man out is, of course, the 1938 57S Bugatti (*centre right*), the absolute antithesis of cheap unitary tinware, classical and bespoke to the Nth degree, and only just endowed with hydraulic brakes. It was also just about the fastest "street" machine one could buy in those days.

Tens the body was welded to a platform, the latter being integral with the chassis proper.

Perhaps the most advanced of all the pre-war unitaries was, however, J.A. Grégoire's Amilcar Compound, first seen at the 1937 Paris Salon. This showed what could be done by a combination of inspired metallurgy and the new idiom. The floor pan, firewall, windshield supports, door stills, and front cross-member were all of light alloy, the result being a four-seater sedan with a 1,185-cc engine, the whole thing weighing only 0.8 tons, where 1 ton was the norm for the class. Even more remarkable, the power unit itself was an obsolete side-valve four to which no lightening techniques had been applied. The Grégoire, alas, was to have a chequered career, and probably less than fifteen hundred cars of all types were made to the designer's own ideas. The post-war Dyna-Panhard, its best-known descendant, was heavily modified by Panhard's design staff.

The automobile of the 1930s looked rather as if it had been designed by parsimonious accountants for moronic owners. A surplus of chromium plate was no substitute for fine workmanship, and under-hood finish was a thing of the past. Styling had ousted craftsmanship. With a few honourable exceptions, the vehicle was not fun to drive, and from a purely technical standpoint a 1939 model cannot be termed revolutionary in relation to what the same money would buy in 1930. What must stand to its credit, though, is that – used in the manner for which it was designed – it worked astonishingly well and would go on doing so for many years.

Semi-unitary construction on the De Soto Airflow, 1934. Here we have such considerations as a perfect aerodynamic shape – designer Carl Breer based his design on a study of bird and aeroplane flight – plus, once again, the need to accommodate all seats within the wheel-base. We have come a long way from 1929 in other respects. Moving the passengers forward involves shifting the engine over the front axle centre-line, and also fitting it into a sloping nose with high streamline fenders which necessitate an alligator hood. It also involved mounting the radiator laterally, an idea of more questionable merit. What is even more interesting is the all-steel girder framework, in effect a species of birdcage on which the body panels were hung. This took some of the strain off the "chassis", hence Chrysler were able to use side-frame rails which were much lighter and shallower than those on conventional cars. Even if the Chrysler and De Soto Airflows were not fully unitary in the Citroën or Lancia sense, they had one important advantage, and one which helped the Corporation to survive the less than enthusiastic reception accordes their "leap in the dark". Body panels were few in number; essentially, there were three: the top and the two sides. Further, they could be standardized throughout the full Airflow range. Future trends were anticipated by incorporating the main differences between Chrysler and De Soto – both dimensionally and in styling detail – into the front-end sheet-metal section from the windshield forward.

3

BODIES – BEAUTIFUL
AND OTHERWISE

At first sight, the story of coachwork in the 1930s is, once again, one of consolidation.

There were, outwardly, no new elements. Stylists – if not under that label – had existed long before Lawrence P. Fisher brought Harley Earl to work at General Motors in 1926. Unitary construction was as old as the automobile itself; many horse-drawn carriages had, indeed, no chassis in the accepted sense. What happened in the 1930s – and to a far greater extent in the first post-Second World War years – was that the work of chassis engineer and body designer coalesced to produce a new generation of automobile.

As we have seen, true unitaries were as yet uncommon. There is a tendency to swell their ranks by attaching a unitary label to the DKW, for instance, but this design featured a simple twin-rail backbone with outriggers. The major supporters of the new idiom in 1939 amounted to General Motors's two European houses (Vauxhall and Opel), Citroën in France, Lancia in Italy, and Hanomag in Germany. J.A. Grégoire's Amilcar was made in insignificant numbers only, while Morris and Renault were still hedging their bets (one unitary type apiece, with a wide range of conventionally-engineered cars as well). As for the latest Hillman Minx, announced on the eve of war, the principal beneficiaries of this, for some time to come, would be members of the Allied fighting services.

Stylistic integration had, however, come a long way since 1920 and was destined to make far more dramatic strides between 1930 and 1942. If we take General Motors's Cadillac Division as a leader (which it was in more senses than one), an intriguing comparison may be drawn between the 353-series Eight of 1930 and the Sixty Special of some nine years later. Hindsight and the collector mentality have ordained that the former is beautiful and the latter just another phase in the stylistic round of Detroit. That distinguished historian Maurice D. Hendry, however, puts it better, labelling the early-thirties cars as "cosmetic" and the later ones as "functional".

Say what one wishes, the 1930 car is still a combination, albeit a well-balanced one, of chassis and body. Integration is limited to the line of hood and belt, even if the fenders, with those almost mandatory wells for the dual sidemounts, complement the ensemble of, say, a "Madame-X" sedan by Fleetwood with the slant windshield. Radiator, bumpers, headlamps, running board, and spare wheels remain separate entities. The luggage accommodation is a shameless appendage; the primitive, unsightly, folding trunk rack, a stylist's despair. Only Packard ever managed to make a successful feature out of it.

Compare it with the Sixty Special shape. Gone is that uncompromis-ing radiator; it has been supplanted by a grille which blends into the front fender line, even if that complex pattern of chromium-plated bars has yet to spill over into the front apron. The headlamps are already receding into the fenders, and running boards have all but disappeared. Not only is there more room for baggage; it lives in an integral projection at the rear of the body, which forms a continuous line, apart from a notchback incorporated in the interests of rear-seat headroom. Bumpers may still pursue a fairly independent existence, but one feels that, at any moment, they may be sucked into the existing frontal ensemble. One is right: this will happen in 1942. As for the spare wheel – the customer can still specify sidemounts if he must, but why bother? There's plenty of room in that big trunk. Like it or not, the wire wheels have given way to plain discs, easier to clean and entirely viable now that improved sound-damping techniques have eliminated the characteristic clangour of those old Michelins on the 1919 Citroën and its contemporaries.

The separate chassis on both these Cadillacs are more rigid than those of many of the opposition. Yet the concept is far more unified than, say, the latest chassis-less Morris Ten with its separate headlamps and conventionally-shaped fenders. We have come a long way since 1914.

Initially, of course, an automobile manufacturer was a chassis maker. As likely as not, he had no interest in bodies. As late as 1910, Renault made few, if any, themselves, and Fiat tended to buy theirs out, even if their basic tourers were standardized. Mercedes owned their carriage shops at Sindelfingen, separate from the main works at Stuttgart. Austin were exceptional in that, even in 1908, "the whole of the carriage work is carried out in our own factory, where, with the aid of the latest and most efficient plant, we are able to fit any type of body the customer may prefer". They were also prepared to "send our carriage designer to confer with and advise anyone not able to visit the works" – surely a case of gilding the lily, when the catalogue already offered a choice of one roadster, seven phaetons, and all of five distinct varieties in the formal idiom.

In effect, Austin were running a custom body shop because they had the facilities. One cannot imagine Herbert Austin sanctioning a body on a rival chassis, though his neighbours, the Lanchester Motor Company, would so oblige customers on occasion. And this "separate" philosophy would outlive even the unifying influences of the stylist. The manufacturers of 1920 showed little interest in bodies, and their successors were content to farm out a surprising proportion of what appeared to be their own responsibility.

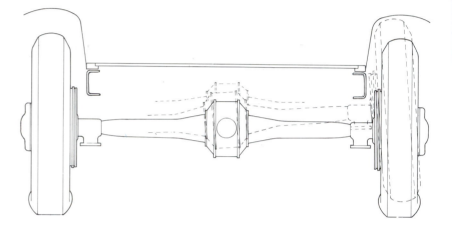

The 1934 Morris Ten (*top left*) and similarly rated 1938 Rover (*centre left*) are to a great extent look-alikes, thanks to bodies of the same make. Rover's cheapest sedans, like almost all Morris's, came from Pressed Steel at Oxford. A lot more handwork went into the Rover, a quality offering costing £248 ($1,240), some £70 ($350) more than was asked for the older Morris. It wasn't until 1938 that Morris would switch to the pushrod overhead valves found on every Rover since 1929. Oddly, though, it is Morris who offer hydraulic brakes: Rover would stay with rod-operated mechanicals until well after the war. The 3½-litre Jaguar (*bottom*) is actually a 1947 model, but the post-war improvements are minor and invisible in this picture; William Lyons's shapes were quite as ageless as Rover's contemporary sports sedans (which they made themselves) and even better proportioned.

It had a top speed of over 90 mph (145 km/h), a comfortable cruising speed of 80 (130 km/h), and an engine life in excess of 100,000 miles (160,000 km) at the price of a daunting thirst (16 mpg or 17.8 lit/100). That the 1938 Cadillac 75 limousine (*top right*) consumed even more fuel mattered little to the customers. Here were all the latest refinements, including coil-spring independent front suspension (all Jaguars made up to 1948 had beam axles) and the brand-new column shift. The 141-in (3.6 m) wheel-base made it an eight-seater.

Bentley under Rolls-Royce management, 1934. It isn't really fair to call the 3½-litre, here seen (*top*) with sedanca coupé body for four, a tuned 20/25 Rolls-Royce, though the engine is a twin-carburettor version of the Royce and the four-speed synchromesh transmission with its right-hand shift is authentic Derby, along with the famous mechanical servo brakes. The performance was in another class altogether: while the 20/25 was flat out at 70 mph (112 km/h), the 110-hp Bentley was good for 90 (145 km/h) and returned a surprising 20 mpg (14 lit/100). The manufacturer's drawing (*opposite, centre right*) is for the guidance of coachbuilders – in the best Rolls-Royce tradition there were no factory bodies – and shows the permitted clearances between axle and rear seat, and wheel arches and wheels. The rules were strict – an accompanying rider stated that if the car was intended for use with snow chains, an extra half-inch (1.25 cm) of clearance must be allowed over the arches. Also marked up for the body builder is the chassis plan view (*bottom*), of especial interest as illustrating the wastefulness of the old long-hooded classic layout. Wheel-base is 126 in (3.2 m, or 6 in/15.2 cm shorter than a 20/25 Rolls-Royce), but though the 96 in (2.4 m) reserved for the body is exclusive of trunk space, one has effectively to deduct 14 in (35.5 cm) for the firewall. The engine's position well back in the frame is also clearly visible.

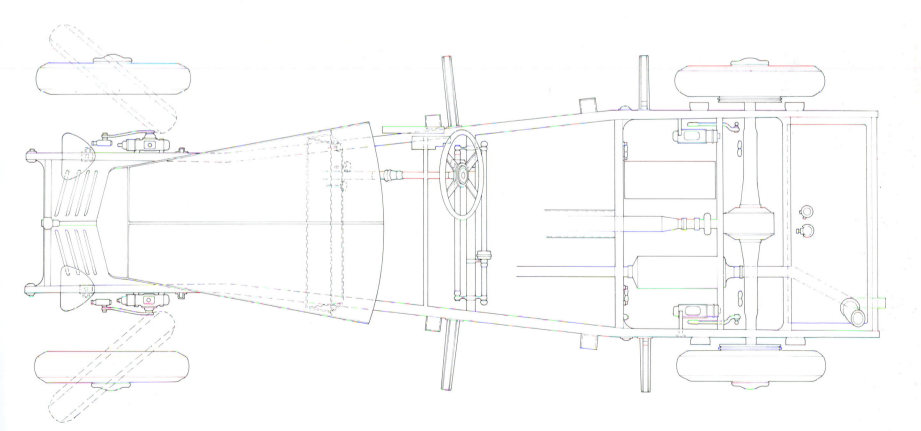

In the interim period before the introduction of their fully integral *traction avant* in 1934, Citroën switched to a "monoshell" form of body construction, here seen on their inexpensive 8CV 1.5-litre sedan of 1933. Since a separate chassis (*below*) was still used, other body types could be fitted, and small-volume production rendered monoshell methods unnecessary for these.

Here the various stages of Citroën's welded-up construction can be seen (*right*). First the two side panels, with sills but not as yet doors, are joined to the complete rear section. Then the top and the structural arch of the firewall are added, while the third phase embraces the dash and floor. Finally, the doors are fitted, though on some variants there was also an integral projecting trunk at the rear, not seen in this sequence. The structure was extremely rigid and could withstand major crashes. An interesting aspect of this form of construction was the metal overlap between the sections, used to strengthen the various welds. In addition to this 8CV body, also used on "light" editions of the 10CV and 15CV cars, there was also a three-window variation for 10s and 15s. Such expensive processes were, of course, only viable for long runs, and 1933 was not a time for such structural experiments, even in the case of a firm with a potential of maybe seventy thousand identical sedans a year. Probably less than twenty thousand of this two-window type were produced.

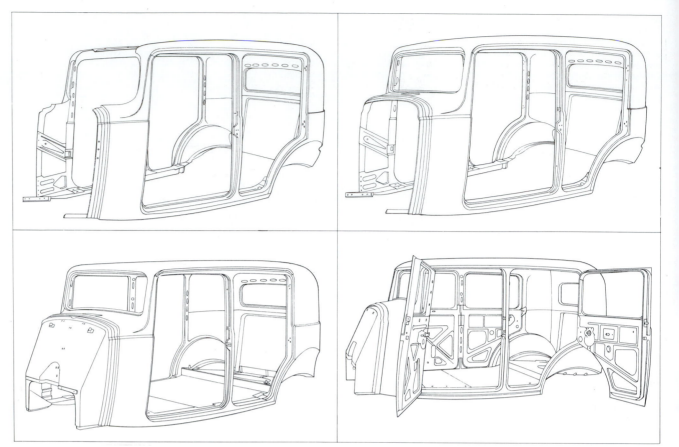

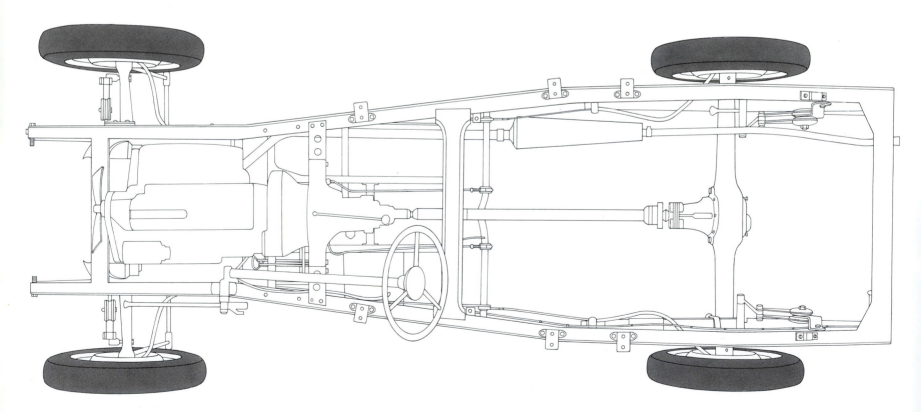

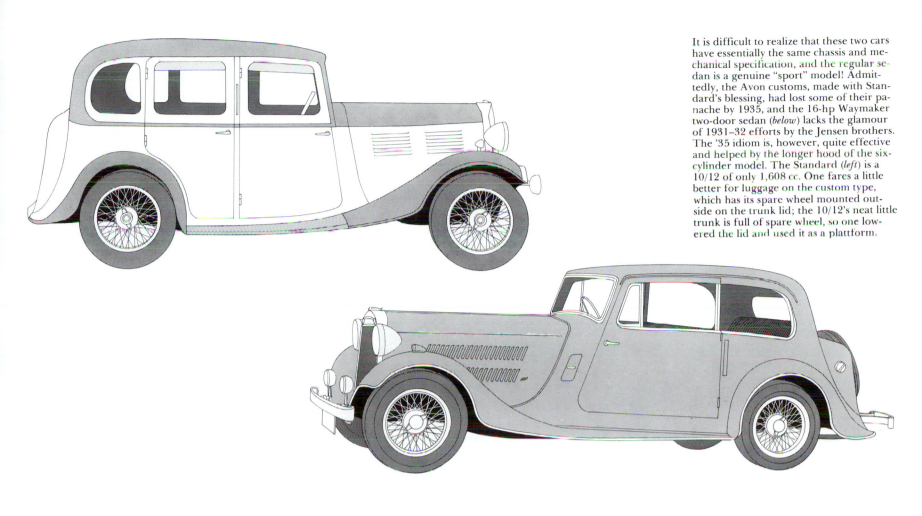

It is difficult to realize that these two cars have essentially the same chassis and mechanical specification, and the regular sedan is a genuine "sport" model! Admittedly, the Avon customs, made with Standard's blessing, had lost some of their panache by 1935, and the 16-hp Waymaker two-door sedan (*below*) lacks the glamour of 1931–32 efforts by the Jensen brothers. The '35 idiom is, however, quite effective and helped by the longer hood of the six-cylinder model. The Standard (*left*) is a 10/12 of only 1,608 cc. One fares a little better for luggage on the custom type, which has its spare wheel mounted outside on the trunk lid; the 10/12's neat little trunk is full of spare wheel, so one lowered the lid and used it as a platform.

In the luxury sporting field, of course, bodies were of interest, whoever made them. W.O. Bentley, the Lyles of Invicta fame, and (especially) Gabriel Voisin were apt to tear up the official warranty if the end-product came out too heavy. Voisin denounced the American-style roadster in ringing terms and compared a car without luggage accommodation to "a weapon with no ammunition". But even in the 1930s, a "factory" body meant little more than a body built in series to a factory-approved specification, sold off the showroom floor with the chassis maker's guarantee. General Motors's cheaper coachwork was the physical responsibility of their Fisher Division, the specialized Fleetwood branch handling the costlier Cadillacs and La Salles. Ford drew heavily on such "trade" firms as Briggs and Murray; in 1936, it was estimated that the former company handled sixty-two per cent of Ford contracts, with twenty-two per cent going to Murray and most of the rest to Budd in Philadelphia. Other important Briggs customers were Chrysler (who would eventually absorb them), Graham, Hudson, and Packard. These American coachbuilders lived off the industry, just as did some of the major British houses – Charlesworth, for instance, and Carbodies. For the time being, coachbuilders would remain independent, though Nash had already solved their body problems by buying their main supplier, Seaman of Milwaukee.

The big trade coachbuilders were, of course, geared to longish runs. When Murray landed Ford's coupé contract in 1935, it may have seemed small pickings by contrast with Briggs's orders for sedans, but that year, Ford were good for close to a million units, and that meant a potential of one hundred coupés alone every working hour. Such a situation, inevitably, called for a two-way guarantee. The chassis maker had to be able to sell the cars as well. Hence, the ingredients of disaster

were at hand, and disaster would supervene once the body specialists switched to unitary hulls.

For smaller runs, different arrangements were required. The chassis maker might be anxious to pad his catalogue, but how to do it when the additional style had a potential of, perhaps, one hundred units out of a model-year run of maybe twenty-five thousand? Setting up jigs in his own shops was hardly viable; far less so would it be to farm the job out to one of the giant press-work specialists. And in these days of all-steel construction and higher amortization levels, a run of at least ten thousand was called for, spread over three years at the maximum.

Thus, we encounter a new class of "tame" coachbuilder. German factories drew their cabriolets from Deutsch, Drauz, Gläser, and Karmann, with Salmons-Tickford as the British equivalent of this quartette. During the 1930s, this latter firm would build catalogued styles for BSA, Daimler, Hillman, Lanchester, MG, Rover, Standard, Triumph, Vauxhall, and Wolseley. In Italy, Fiat used Garavini and Viotti, among others.

Vauxhall, perhaps, show the body policy of the 1930s at its most typical. More interestingly still, they were one of the few firms which successfully effected the transformation from carriage-trade to big league. When General Motors took over in 1925, the factory was under-employed in relation to an annual potential of only fifteen hundred cars. In 1939, they were good for forty thousand, a figure they would surely have achieved but for the war. And before they went unitary, they prided themselves on their diversity of body styles.

Yet all they made themselves at Luton were the regular sedans. The four-passenger Light Six coupés, listed as factory bodies, were, in fact, made by Pressed Steel at Oxford. Two-door convertibles were usually

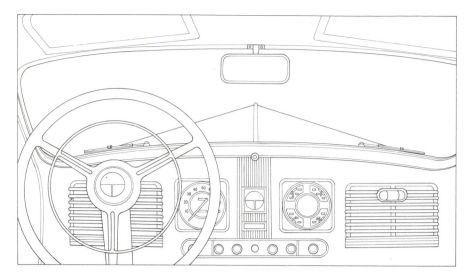

The 1938 Chrysler Imperial Eight marks the triumph of styling over most other considerations, though at least the facia (*top left*) contains instruments of recognizable shape. The sectioning of dials into four quarters (amps, fuel, oil pressure, water temperature) is a favourite space-saver of the period, and preferable to the later configuration (a fuel gauge, plus "idiot lights" for the other three!) The front end (*top right*) reflects the horizontal-bar motifs to which all American makers were addicted in 1937 and 1938. In Britain, of course, General Motors's local branch, Vauxhall, was the mainstay of the local custom-body industry. The 1933–34 AS-type Light Six Stratford sporting four-seater (*bottom*) by Whittingham and Mitchel of London had quite a lot of charm and cost only about £30 ($150) more than a stock sedan. The coachbuilder was not seduced by the snob appeal of sidemounts and managed to convey an illusion of greater length by extending the hood right back to windshield level.

The 1931 sixteen-cylinder Cadillac roadster (*opposite, top right*) looks every inch a thoroughbred, with its long hood (note the then-fashionable doors), scalloped fenders, sidemounts, and wire wheels. Proportions are near perfect, and only a dedicated utilitarian could complain that there is far too much car for two people. At the other end of the scale are two later American solutions for big families on vacation or in pursuit of heavy shopping. Ford's 1939 V8 Woody (*opposite, top left*) was probably the first station wagon to sell in big quantities. Bodies shared no panels with other styles and thus cost more to make: they also called for frequent revarnishing and were ill-suited for tropical climes. Some quiverful families preferred the seven-passenger sedan, a lengthened edition of the stock article, with jump seats. Unwieldy it certainly was: the 1939 P6 Plymouth (*bottom*) had its wheel-base extended from 112 in (2.8 m) to 132 in (3.4 m).

assigned to Salmons-Tickford, though earlier ones came from Martin Walter of Folkestone, plus a handful from Grose (Northampton), and Vauxhall's "tame" coachbuilder, the London-based Grosvenor. Sport sedans, by Holbrook of Coventry, Palmer of Dover, and even Bertelli of Aston Martin fame, figured in sundry catalogues, while all the four-door convertibles were Martin Walter's well-loved Winghams, also listed by Hillman and Daimler-Lanchester. Holbrook also produced a small number of sports tourers, though the majority of these came from Whittingham and Mitchel, a London house specializing in sportier styles. Those whose tastes ran to a traditional roadster or tourer could have it as late as 1935–36, from Duple, whose usual line of business was bus bodies, many of them for Vauxhall-built Bedford chassis. It is easy to understand why Martin Walter switched to commercial coachbuilding when Vauxhall elected to dispense with separate chassis.

"Tame" coachbuilders were an asset in those difficult days. Gordon of Birmingham built only on Austin chassis, Cunard on Morris, and until they were taken over by Standard after the Second World War, Mulliners of Birmingham worked mainly for Daimler. Standard themselves padded their range with attractive sporting bodies commissioned from New Avon of Warwick. It all helped make elegance and variety as painless as synchromesh – and still kept the cost accountants from complaining.

Some styles, of course, could not be fitted into the new idiom, however high their sales potential. Most important of these was the original woody-type station wagon, still regarded as a commercial vehicle, though usually fitted to a regular passenger chassis. Its social acceptance would be a wartime phenomenon. Hence, sales were low – the usual clients were ranches, hotels, and the Stately Homes of the Old World, where the woody doubled as transport for guns to the butts and servants to the village hop. Worse still, its constructional methods militated against every principle of press-work. At best, it shared cowl, windshield, and rear fenders with sedans or coupés.

Thus, woodies were farmed out. Ford, with the advantage of a factory-owned wood mill, made all the components but had Murray assemble them. When the Depression struck, a Kentucky firm took over the timberware. Chrysler bought from the Indiana-based US Body and Forging Company, while General Motors, for all the Fisher family's timber interests, were still using three outside suppliers in 1940. By this time, business had picked up – Ford alone disposed of thirteen thousand wagons that year, so they were able to reopen their mill and dispense with outside help. Chrysler, likewise, had switched to a fully-owned subsidiary, though even then the bits were sent to Detroit for assembly.

These complicated minor operations were necessitated by the spread of press-work: a good body shop accustomed to composite construction could easily have coped with the woodies in the 1920s, had there been a demand. But times had changed.

The big American operations – Briggs, Budd, Fisher, and Murray – were now matched by European ventures such as Pressed Steel in Britain, Chausson in France, and Ambi-Budd in Germany. These, like all the American companies save Fisher, were independent of the car makers; Pressed Steel, launched as a Morris exclusive in 1927, broadened its base after 1930, when Morris sold his share and let other firms cash in on the benefits of methods which eliminated screw joints and hand-work. Such plants cost money: £2 million ($10 million) of capital and £0.5 million worth of equipment (including a 245-ton press) went into the creation of Pressed Steel's Oxford works, but manufacture was simplified. A Budd-type body's side panels, from windshield post to rear quarter, were pressed out two at a time, and a set of door panels could be produced every twenty seconds. All sections were electrically welded and painted – though not trimmed – before despatch. By 1931, Pressed Steel were supplying Austin, Hillman, Rover, and Wolseley as well as Morris, while at pebk, they would be responsible for either complete bodies or panels for fourteen British factories. In Germany, Ambi-Budd's parallel operation in Berlin built for Adler, Audi, BMW, Ford, Hanomag, and even the up-market Horch.

Inevitably, the cost accountants had their look-in, and some cross-pollination resulted. This went beyond mere badge-engineering: a similarity between Morrises and Wolseleys was to be expected since both firms were part of the same group, but Rover's economy drive included the use of some Hillman Minx panels on their cheapest Tens, the same shape finding its way across the North Sea onto a few of Ambi-Budd's Adlers. By the same token, Berlin's Jupiter sedan, a more attractive shape, was common to four-cylinder Adlers and Hanomags – and also, curiously, to sports models of the Austin Light 12/6! The exotic front-wheel-drive Ruxton, an American ephemeral of 1930, actually used Morris-Wolseley coachwork, cut down to fit the American car's lower build: the rear quarter-lights, which wound down in Britain, had to hinge in transatlantic guise, since otherwise they would have fouled the wheel arches. Sometimes, this standardization would kill a make: Chenard-Walcker's promising 1935 front-wheel-drive sedan failed to win acceptance simply because, in the interests of economy, it used a Chausson-built body identical to that of the new French Ford V8s made in the old Mathis factory.

This system also made for complications in the styling department. Buying from Ambi-Budd or Chausson exonerated the manufacturer from investing in costly body plant. It could, if he wished, spare him the expense of paintwork as well, though many makers preferred to handle this aspect of the job along with the interior trim. At the same time, however, the system landed him with the old headache of amortization – a long run, or else. This was fine if the car sold; if it didn't, he had either to rework the mechanics round the old shape or face a substantial loss. Rootes had more progressive ideas than most of their British rivals, but the failure of their first Pressed Steel effort, the Hillman Wizard Six of 1931, is reflected in the continuance of essentially the same shape right up to 1935.

Unitary construction heightened these problems. Even where a basic body had to be retained for an extra year, a surprising amount could be done with the extremities, while work on engines and running gear was not wholly impeded. Hillman eked out the Wizard catastrophe with three grilles, two fender lines, and two different tail panels, while the suppliers of outside "semi-customs" helped. But once the chassis was built into the body, overall dimensions became constant, as did, for instance, the location of an engine bearer in relation to the firewall. One may suspect that even Citroën were saved by the war: otherwise, how could they have soldiered on into 1955 with no stylistic changes beyond 1952's projecting rear trunk?

The principles of unitary construction have already been discussed, as have the principal pros and cons. But from the standpoint of the body designer – and thus, ultimately, the customer – the big problem was the sheer inflexibility, though this would hit far harder in the post-war years. Further, a disaster could be a two-way one: one could be stuck at one and the same time with defective steering geometry and a shape that was no longer acceptable. The 1948 Step Down Hudsons had passed beyond redemption by chromium plate and minor fender alterations when they were finally scrapped at the end of 1954, while sometimes the public would give a car the thumbs-down before it had time to prove itself. Such a case was Grégoire's big R-type flat-four of 1949: while Hotchkiss, the licencees, certainly lacked the funds to get such an ambitious project off the ground, it is also true that the distaff

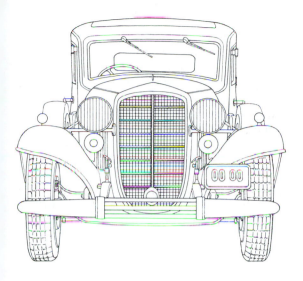

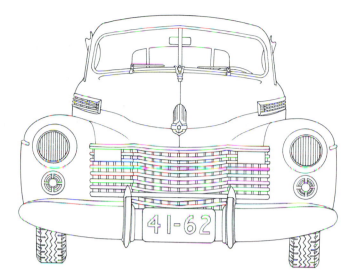

The march of styling, or how the cosmetic evolved into the functional entity. In the front view of the 1933 Cadillac (*left*), the fender skirts are not visible, and in any case, the frontal skirting would be the next stage. Cord influence is, however, detectable in the vee-grille, new on General Motors cars that year, and already, an attempt has been made to pretty-up the bumper. Everything else — headlamps, trumpet horns, and dual sidemounts — is out of doors, and the overslung wipers cannot park out of the driver's sight. On the 1941 Cadillac (*right*), however, there are very few excrescences: the pattern of heavy chromium-plated bars has spread from the grille into the fenders and is bidding fair to overwhelm the fully recessed headlamps. Likewise, the bumper is merging into the grille. All the other excrescences are out of sight, the spare wheel having been banished to the trunk.

The luggage problem (*bottom right*). The luggage grid (trunk rack) was an unsightly object at the best of times and tended to foul the spare wheel. On this 1932 Austin, a well for the spare wheel has been incorporated in the rear panel, but it was left to Packard (page 136, *bottom*) to make a distinctive feature of the excrescence.

Tidying up could destroy individuality, and Austin's 1935 grille was scarcely beautiful. One of the casualties of this clean-up was the radiator filler cap (*bottom left*), which went under the hood. This meant eventually that many a mascot was no longer functional, though there was some compensation in knowing that, when you opened the hood, you could top up radiator, sump, and battery at one sitting.

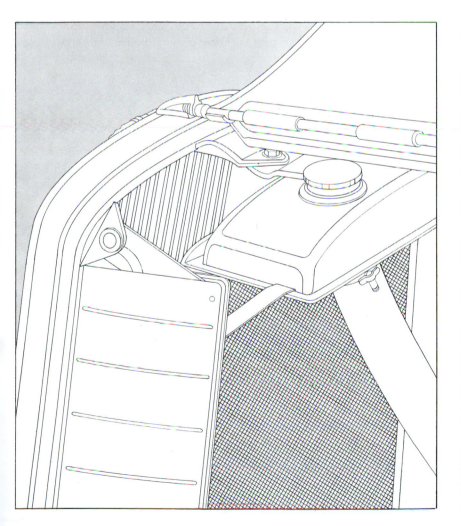

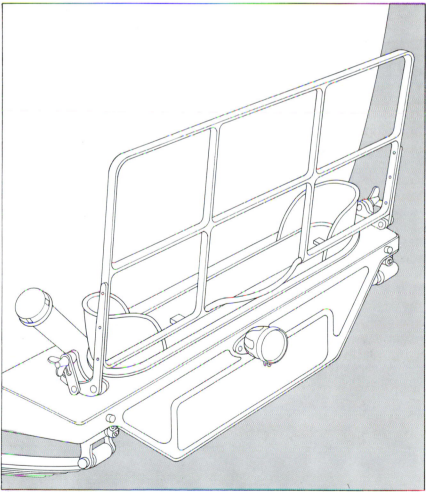

Diversity in coachwork. You really needed the long hood of a straight-eight to exploit the 1929 Cord idiom, and Chrysler's 1931 CD-type filled the bill admirably. The factory provided both the coupé (*opposite, top*) and the convertible (*top right*), though the fancy touches – dual sidemounts, tyre covers, and wire wheels – were extras. You could have a radio also on the closed models. On such styles, unfortunately, Americans still clung to the discriminatory rumble seat for extra passengers. Europeans didn't, so Chrysler's English branch offered a more sociable drophead foursome or convertible coupé (*opposite, bottom right*) by Carlton of London for local consumption. By 1939, the Americans had caught up with European thinking, and the result is seen here (*opposite, bottom left*) on Packard's 120 convertible. The firm's conservative styling rendered sidemounts more bearable than they were on Buicks and Cadillacs, though money had been saved by making the same chassis and sheet metal do for both the nine-bearing Super Eight and the less expensive five-bearing 120. The 1940 Nash (*top left*) is of interest as being a fastback at a time when other people were concentrating on trunkbacks – it is also apparent that styling was not taken too seriously at Kenosha.

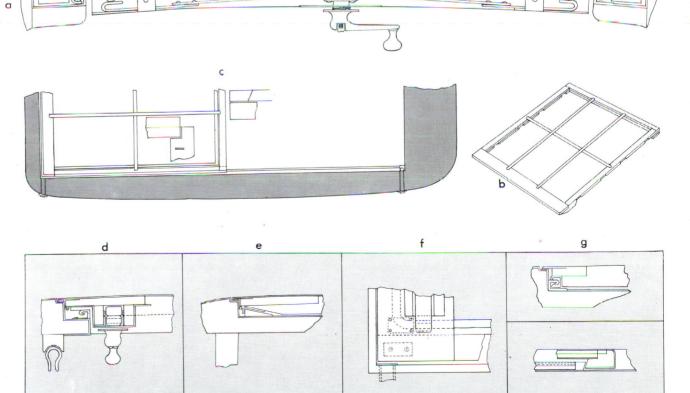

Typically British was the sliding roof (*bottom*); we show here the Saloonood system fitted on some British cars of the period. (*a*) Section through the sliding roof, showing the locking device. (*b*) Perspective view of the assembled sliding panel. (*c*) The roof and sliding panel seen from above. The sliding panel is seen on the left. Sections through various parts of the roof and panel (*d, e, f, g*) show the complicated construction. In a temperate climate it was remarkably leak-proof. One of the first users of a sliding roof were Standard, on the 1931 Big Nine (*centre left*), a lot of car for 1,287 cc, thanks to the British horsepower tax. Understandably, 55 mph (90 km/h) were hard work, but a bonus was the fuel consumption – only 36 mpg (8 lit/100). A safe if limited seller of the 1930s was the inexpensive limousine based on a big family sedan. This happened in most countries, though shown here (*centre right*) is a British example, the 1938 GL type Vauxhall 25 with 3.4-litre overhead-valve six-cylinder engine. Wheel-base was lengthened by 19 in (48 cm), and Grosvenor's custom body used a number of stock panels. If it sounds expensive at £630 ($3,150), remember that Daimler's least expensive formal carriage listed at close on £1,000 ($5,000).

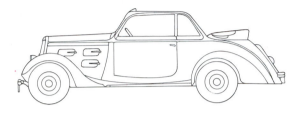

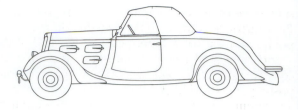

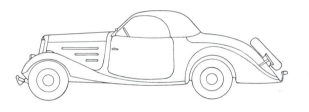

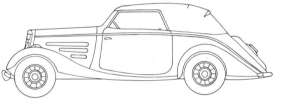

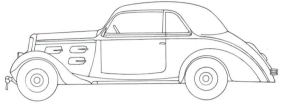

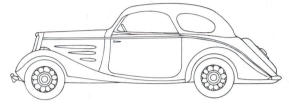

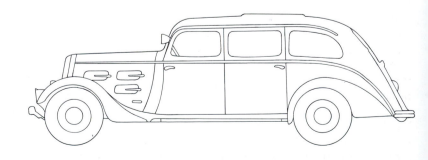

All the same model, 1935 1.7-litre four-cylinder Peugeot 401s. Let's say the social equivalent of a Standard Twelve in England or a DU Dodge in the United States. Technical specifications are constant, though there is a choice of wheel-base lengths to allow the French to indulge their passion for *commerciales*, or seven-to-eight-passenger commercial sedans which came to be used to deliver goods during the working week. One from the bottom on the right is what we would now term a hatchback, with an upward-opening tailgate to give a good loading height at the price, maybe, of a knock on the head in passing. These long-chassis jobs, of course, called for lower axle ratios, also used in the very similar MK light truck family, which carried on into 1936 to use up surplus front-end sheet metal, a common habit in the industry.

Most intriguing of all the numerous variants is, however, the *decapotable électrique* (*bottom left*), an anticipation of Ford's legendary 1957 retractable on which the metal top was lowered electrically into a space behind the front seats. Peugeot persisted with this design for several years, but it was too complicated to meet with much success, especially since buyers had

a choice of three different types of orthodox soft-top convertible, including a traditional roadster with the refinement of wind-up windows. (Latterly, you could have a German-style cabrio-limousine as well, in the cheap 202 line made from 1938 onwards). American styling influences are much in evidence, especially in the fastback idiom used for all the sedans, though the low-set headlamps are still exposed and fender treatment remains orthodox. Note also that Detroit-style hood doors are still fashionable in France a good year after American stylists have gone over to speedstreaks. Peugeot also ring the changes on hood louvre design, with a more modern crib of American themes on the sportier bodies. Unlike those other devotees of body styles unlimited, Vauxhall, Peugeot made all their own coachwork. What is even more surprising is that the 401 had only a one-year run, accounting for less than fourteen thousand units, though some panels were common to the smaller 201 and 301 series, and a virtually identical line of bodies sufficed for the six-cylinder 601 at the top of the range. Here Peugeot took a leaf out of Chrysler's book by adding the extra length in the hood, where it did not affect other dimensions.

side objected to its drooping nose. Grégoire later wished he had hired Pininfarina to transform his ugly duckling, but such international cross-pollination was uncommon, even at the end of the forties.

Inflexibility of style was almost a worse handicap. With full unitary construction, the choice lay between two- and four-door sedans, and (in post-woody days) that admirable standby, the station wagon, though any attempt at bulk production of such a car in 1939 would have been financially disastrous. On a small and cheap model, one could sometimes eke out the tooling costs, as did Hillman and Renault, with a light panel delivery van; before the advent of Volkswagen's revolutionary Transporter in 1950, car-type vans were generally acceptable. Convertibles, however, presented a real headache. Without the necessary reinforcement of a steel roof, one was confronted with immediate firewall shake, followed by a speedy demise once rust, a unitary hull's worst enemy, set in. Hence the high mortality rate, and the subsequent astronomical collector-value, of Citroën's beautiful roadsters, discontinued after 1940. Vauxhall and Lancia circumvented the problem by offering chassis-ed versions; the former financing this extravagance by using the construction in their smaller Bedford vans, while the latter could hardly be called a mass-producer at any time and always worked to more modest parameters of output. The Germans – and later Ted Ulrich of Nash – had a more practical solution in the cabrio-limousine, a ragtop with rigid sides. It worked, though it had about as much aesthetic appeal as the *targhe* of the safety-conscious seventies.

The "desire to be different" occupied body departments as deeply as it did the engineers. As long as chassis remained separate entities, one could ring the changes indefinitely on engines, gearboxes, wheelbase lengths, and body styles. Austin's 1934 catalogue embraced over fifty different models, while in the same year, Peugeot's 1.5-litre 301 family came in fourteen styles, from a sporty roadster to a six-seater *familiale* for quiverful Frenchmen. The 1931 Renault catalogue listed seven variations of the pint-sized six-cylinder Mona, six of the indestructible KZ four, ten of the 3.2-litre Viva, and seven of the Nerva, the cheaper of the company's two straight-eights (the vast Reinastella ran to 7.1 litres and was strictly bespoke). In Germany Opel customers must have found life dull when the company went unitary. Five body styles, including a traditional roadster, were available on 1933's 1.2-litre, one of Germany's cheapest cars, but by 1937, the modern Kadett came as a two-door sedan or cabrio-limousine. Even a four-door model would not be added until 1938.

In the United States, of course, variations were almost limitless. Throughout our period, two- and four-door sedans invariably topped the best-seller lists, while roadsters and phaetons had virtually disappeared by 1935. Their successors were the convertible coupés, though oddly, these would retain the uncomfortable and discriminatory rumble seat into 1937–38, possibly because in the days of manually-operated tops, the shorter type was more manageable. Four-passenger "victoria" bodies, though they enjoyed a short vogue in 1932, were less popular, while even rarer was the four-door convertible sedan, a style much favoured by well-heeled Germans. Fixed-head coupés, like the ragtops, clung overlong to the rumble seat, though a favourite variation was the "business" model, on which the rear-deck space was reserved for baggage. Woodies remained rare; Ford's 1929 lead in this field was not immediately followed. Finally, there was a simple extension of the sedan theme – a long-chassis, seven-passenger job using many of the regular panels. If Ford ignored this type and Chevrolet confined its application to their taxicab range, Chrysler and Hudson made quite a few. So, incidentally, did Hillman, Vauxhall, and Austin in Britain, Opel in Germany, and all of France's Big Three. In the United States one could afford to drop an individual style for a season – neither Chevrolet nor

Dodge, for instance, listed a convertible in 1939 – but one dared not abdicate altogether. The Joneses of the automobile world, be they traders or actual owners, expect to be catered for all the time.

We shall discuss purely national trends in a later chapter, but if the decade had an "in" style, it was surely the convertible, call it a cabriolet or a drophead coupé. Never a big seller, for all the growing sex-absorption of press departments, it nonetheless occupied that "status" later to be usurped by the hardtop, the more luxurious station wagons, and the *targa*-type near-cabriolet. Germany was the convertible's stronghold, and undoubtedly some of the best workmanship and weather protection came from there. Internally lined tops were regular practice, though one paid for these in avoirdupois: Karmann's four-passenger body on the small Adler Trumpf Junior chassis – a standard sedan turned the scales at about 1,760 lb (800 kg) – boasted a top said to weigh nearly 110 lb (50 kg). All types of variation were available, as a study of contemporary Mercedes-Benz catalogues will attest. Of their offerings, the A was the sportiest, a two-passenger affair innocent of rumble, though occasionally a sideways- facing opera seat would be provided for a third crew member. The Mercedes-Benz B was a sobre two-door, four-window affair, while the C was the same thing, only more intimate, with blind rear quarters. The D had four doors, and the F – supplied only for real heavies such as the Nürburg straight-eight and the vast 7.7-litre Grosser – was a full formal, ideal for a trip to the opera. As this one was intended for chauffeur drive, unfurling of the massive top could safely be left to this unhappy hireling.

Elsewhere two-door four-passenger types predominated, offering intimacy and an individual line at the price of negligible rearward vision. (This may explain why contemporary British rallyistes preferred to run even unsporting models in the "open-car" category – conducting such a vehicle backwards was a nightmare, especially in the early 1930s, when long hoods and slit-type windshields were all the rage). Power tops, though tried by a few custom coachbuilders as early as 1936, did not become general practice even in the United States until 1940–41. They never spread across the Atlantic, though Peugeot would anticipate the ingenious metal retractables of a far later era with their *décapotable électrique*, a sensation of the 1934 Paris Salon. By contrast, the three-position top enjoyed considerable snob value, giving a sedanca effect in the intermediate position, and offering, as Standard asserted in a 1935 advertisement, "three cars in one".

Roadster-type bodies in the American idiom were rarer, though they had a following in France, always more susceptible to the ideas of Detroit. Citroën, Peugeot, and Renault all offered them in 1938–39; so, in a higher price bracket, did AC and Triumph on the other side of the Channel. The rumble seat, however, remained uncomfortable, even when Triumph sought to give it some added status on their post-war 1800. This curiosity featured windows in the deck lid, permitting the latter component to double as a second cowl, in the best Duesenberg tradition. The "foursome drophead", however, would remain popular until its ranks were decimated by post-war unitary influences. Nineteen British manufacturers listed such a style in 1935, and sixteen were still doing so three years later. The choice was wide: from the Standard 8 at £149 ($745), with rear seats suitable only for small children, up to £1,600 ($8,000) worth of V12 Lagonda. There was similar market coverage in France, while Germany fared even better, with everything from two-seaters to cabrio-limousines.

On its way out – and dead by 1933 – was one of the prime fads of the later 1920s, the Weymann system of flexible fabric construction. It reached its zenith in 1929, though Germans were not over-enthusiastic about it, and in the United States only Stutz saw fit to catalogue bodies of this type. Other surprising abstainers were Citroën (apposite, since

Fresh air and fun in the 1930s. A good halfway solution was the German cabrio-limousine, a stock sedan with a full-length roll-top but fixed sides. The 1938 Opel Kadett (*top left*) was one of the cheapest in Europe, at RM 2,150 or less than £150 ($750). Its main failing was that the lowered top impeded the driver's rearward view. The same went for contemporary full cabriolets like the 1935 Mercedes-Benz 290 (*top right*). This one was truly convertible, but the price paid for excellent Teutonic workmanship was excessive weight.

By comparison, three open British cars with demountable side curtains. The 1932 Morris Minor (*centre left*) (this is the rare early-1932 with fluted top to the radiator shell), had restricted vision with the top up, a failing also of the 1931 2-litre supercharged Lagonda (*centre right*). Its shallow windshield would have called for 'blind flying' techniques on a wet day. On a 120-inch (3 m) wheel-base there was plenty of room for four. Finally, pure traditional (*bottom*): only the painted radiator shell and rear trunk (dedicated wholly to the spare wheel!) mark this Austin Ten as a 1935–36. Aerodynamics meant nothing to Herbert Austin — eye-level vision was one of his obsessions.

(*Top*) The 1937 11 *légère* Citroën as an elegant roadster. Being unitary, it lost structural strength through the absence of a roof. It was also rust-prone and the mortality rate was formidable: Citroën quietly dropped the style after 1939

Also a structural headache was the lightweight Weymann fabric body, here seen (*bottom*) dissected. This angular example is an early 1924 effort by Rover, but the principle was still much in evidence in 1930–31. Upper left in the insert, the window frame. Below it, a door detail showing the window mechanism, and on the right, a cross-section of the complete door. *a* is the exterior covering in coloured fabric, *b* the cotton wadding used as insulation, *c* a waterproofed fabric lining on both sides, and *d* the interior trim. The window glass (*e*) dropped into cloth-covered rubber tubing (*f*). Initially, there was nothing to squeak or rattle, and nothing heavy either, but fabric did not take kindly to any extremes of climate, and as the wooden framing "worked", the whole elaborate structure came quietly apart. In England and France, Weymann strongholds, a common sight of the mid-thirties was a fabric sedan with cracks in the outer finish, through which soggy wadding was visible. The medium was, however, much favoured for big sporting sedans, not solely on grounds of weight: it eliminated the drumming from a large and noisy power unit. Many 4½-litre Bentleys were so bodied, but few survive in this form. The majority ended up as "replica" sport tourings "of the school of Vanden Plas", and who should blame the owners? All too many of the originals were ugly, with minimal vision in any direction.

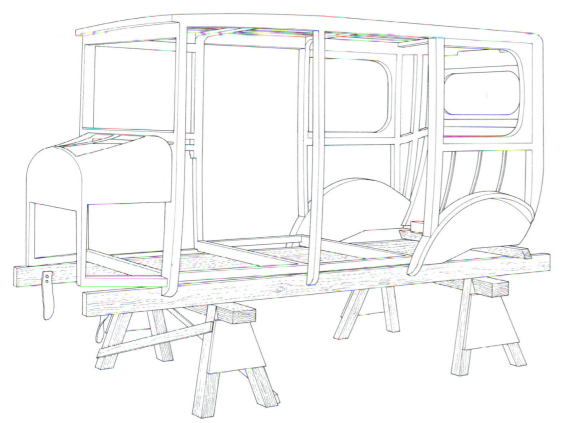

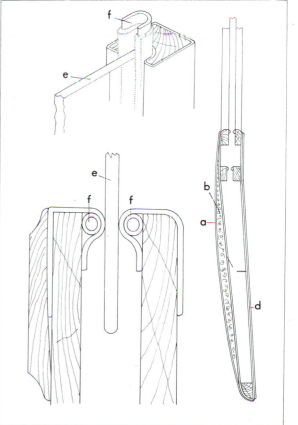

they were pioneers of all-steel construction), and Singer, who had tried it early on and found it wanting. For a while though, it was almost mandatory with other French makers. In England Jowett and Rover were perhaps its staunchest supporters. The *système* Weymann had its good points: it was appreciably lighter than a coach-built body, its leather covering was easier to clean and was fade-proof, and drumming (a bugbear of early closed coachwork) was entirely eliminated. A well-constructed specimen would withstand considerable abuse, but cheap, mass-produced copies were less solidly made and disintegrated rapidly, a familiar sign of decay being tufts of wadding projecting from torn fabric. With the demise of flexible fabric construction went the classic "in-style" of the final vintage years, the sportsman's coupé. The combination of a shallow windshield, a high waist-line, blind rear quarters, and (on more expensive specimens) non-functional plated landau irons lent the style a certain elegance. It was, however, of questionable use to the sportsman, since the impressive-looking rear trunk opened from the top – awkward in all conscience, but quite useless in conjunction with a rear-mounted spare wheel.

Fabric's only survival point was in Germany, where it lingered on as the outer skin of cut-price babies like the DKW-Front. On these it served to keep weight down, enabling four people to be carried at reasonable speeds on 684 cc and 16 bhp. A few Adlers and small German Fiats were also seen with fabric bodies, as was Ford-Cologne's attempt at a proto-Volkswagen in 1935. Despite a price as low as RM 1,850, *Der Wagen für Jedermann* never caught on. It was not, one suspects, the fabric: *Jedermann*, unlike John Smith or Marcel Dupont,

already expected independent front suspension, even in the bargain basement.

In any case, fabric interfered with another important aspect of the new desire to be different – bright colours. In these days of vivid and constantly-changing hues as an accepted means of eking out an obsolescent shape, one tends to forget that Ford was not the only early mass-producer wedded to a solitary shade of black. So was Dodge, even in 1925, when Hudsons, Essexes, most Hupmobiles, and all Studebaker sedans were blue. Buick essayed at least a degree of variety by assigning different colour schemes to individual models, and Citroën had injected a spark of brightness with the punning lemon-yellow of his 5CV runabouts. But generally, outside the realm of the sporty and the bespoke, dark shades and uninspired colour separations (in nine cases out of ten, the "second colour" was black) were the order of the day. Memorable in their time had been Rover's pseudo-sporting 9/20s: they were no balls of fire at any time, but their two-toning, in "strawberries and cream", made them more attractive than Austins, Morrises, or Singers. A further innovation of the 1920s was the "pen nib" colour separation, with a tapering flash of the second colour running down the top of the hood. Indelibly associated in British minds with William Lyons's Austin Swallow sedans, it was in fact the creation of American stylist Ralph Roberts from the famous Le Baron Studios. This led to better things and away from the primitive two-tone concepts of earlier years.

Alas! the best one could do with fabric was to finish fenders and wheels in bright shades – reds and greens were favourites – and add such touches as coloured steering wheels. Now, however, belt mould-

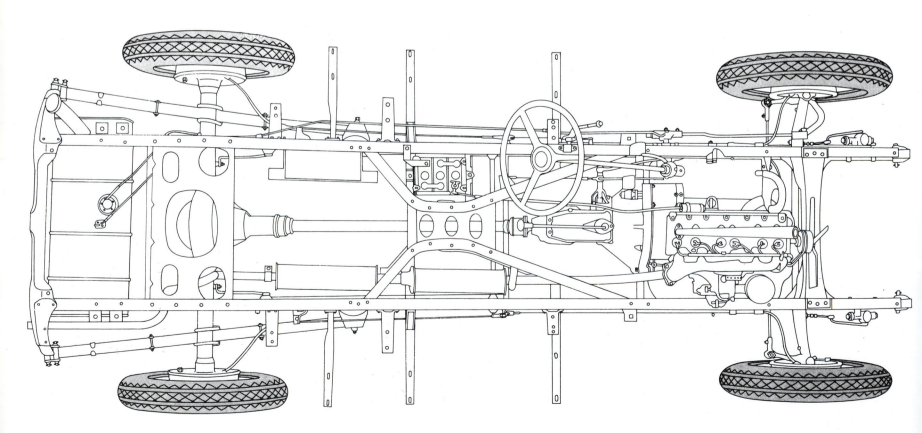

State of the art, 1932. The Essex chassis (*opposite*) is still a fairly simple affair. Americans did not need unitary construction, which was too inflexible for the wide choice of bodies and biennial styling changes characteristic of the period. In essence, we have the same set-up as on the 1930 Volvo 652 shown on page 21, but with one variation, the central cruciform bracing pioneered by Hotchkiss in 1921 and first seen on a production car (the Cord L29) eight years later. The Essex's frame is narrower than the Volvo's, hence the outriggers to serve as body mounts, regular practice on tubular backbone layouts. The battery is also still parked inside the frame, one of the irritants of the period, since a seat (the driver's, in this case) had to be slid back and a hatch raised to get at it. (Lifting the hood and topping up the battery has become a complete routine by this time, to be carried out every time one refuelled.) One might think the Essex's cable-operated brakes a retrograde step after the Volvo's hydraulics, but not everyone trusted the newfangled arrangements, and rubber piping was not as durable in 1932 as it is today. (It took the Second World War to teach the industry all about synthetics.) Note however that the brake drums are of fairly generous proportions, and these, allied to the wire wheels which were pretty general practice in the United States between 1932 and 1934, gave reasonable cooling and, therefore, freedom from fade. Not that the average motorist worried unduly about this prevailing 1950s problem in the days when 50 mph (80 km/h) was considered a high cruising velocity for the family sedan. The contemporary and brand-new Ford vee-eight was good for over 80 mph (130 km/h), but how many people who bought the model cared?

When six-cylinder cars were first marketed in the 1904–07 period, they were conceived as town carriages and sold on flexibility. Here two sixes from the beginning of our period—but from opposite sides of the Atlantic—show just how versatile the idiom had become. In fact, however, both the 1929 Essex (*bottom*)—very much the same car was still being offered in 1931, styling differences apart—and the 1933 Wolseley Hornet Special (*top*) had their roots in the laity's dislike of shifting. This had bred generation after generation of small and cheap sixes in the United States since 1915.

The Wolseley is merely the sporting development of Sir William Morris's archetype of the pint-sized six, launched in 1930 and combining small car proportions (and, in Britain, annual tax) with the ability to do almost everything in high gear.

One should not, therefore, be seduced by the Wolseley's obviously bespoke appearance into regarding it as anything more than a "sporty" automobile fabricated from mass-produced components, a formula pioneered in Britain by Cecil Kimber with the M-type MG Midget (1929) and one which has remained largely British ever since. The Essex, by contrast, was the parent Hudson firm's all-time best seller, 1929 being the season in which the group delivered over three hundred thousand cars, more than anyone else save Chevrolet and Ford.

ings grew more ambitious. The modest "streamlining" of the Series II Morris and Wolseley sedans (1935–36) was accentuated by an ingenious belt treatment, especially on the more expensive Wolseleys, though nobody went as far as Renault in 1933, with their strip of darker cellulose running down the firewall from windshield level. It looked better than one might imagine. Such arrangements could, however, work only as long as fenders remained separate entities.

True pastel shades would be a post-war phenomenon. The colours of the 1930s tended to be darker and muddier, variations of a greyish fawn being used by Hillman, Renault, Opel, and Ford, though the last-mentioned firm called it "Cordoba tan". Metallics made their appearance in the United States in 1932. They succeeded, as they were a cheap means of reproducing something hitherto possible only by expensive admixtures of fish scales. On smaller cars, unfortunately, the effect was somewhat meretricious, though Fiat's British importers worked wonders with two-tone browns and greens on *topolino* coupés. Home-market versions, however, retained their sombre monochromes.

This general brightening up of the automobile had much to do with the integration of the stylist into design departments. Not that he was always welcomed. Styling was a dirty word where the elder Ford was concerned, and Herbert Austin was obsessed with eye-level vision – hence the perpendicular lines of his cars right up to 1936. Chrysler alternated between ambitious sallies (1931's Cord-like CD/CM family and 1934's legendary Airflow) and the stolidly dull, with the emphasis laid on engineering. Kaufman T. Keller, who guided the corporation's

destiny for many years, was certainly interested in styling, but his interest tended to be destructive. One of the less probable Keller credos was that all trunks should be able to house a milk churn standing upright, an eccentricity which explains why the outstanding mechanical virtues of the legendary hemi-head vee-eights of a later era were so depressingly cloaked.

Much of a stylist's work, of course, centred round the task of making an obsolescent shape look new. One has only to study the grilles of Hillmans, Renaults, or Standards of the later 1930s to realize that quick visual impact has been used to suggest more dramatic changes than are actually present. The individuality of Gordon Buehrig's much praised (and hastily created) 1935 Auburn front-end should not blind anyone to the truth: from the firewall aft, the car is virtually identical with Al Leamy's commercially unsuccessful 1934 effort! Pontiac's legendary silver streaks started in 1934 as plated fender trims, put there by Franklin Hershey to avoid an otherwise understandable confusion with the previous year's models. By contrast, La Salle's contemporary port-holes, later to become a Buick hallmark, formed part of an "aeronautical" theme by Jules Agramonte, that would become a style leader.

Nor is it fair to say that styling was "invented" either by Harley Earl or by Edsel Ford, whose personal flair had already transformed that company's recently acquired Lincoln from a triumph of engineering over aesthetics into one of America's more handsome automobiles. One of the advantages of using trade coachbuilders was that their designers had a say in the appearance of the end-product – and both Murray and

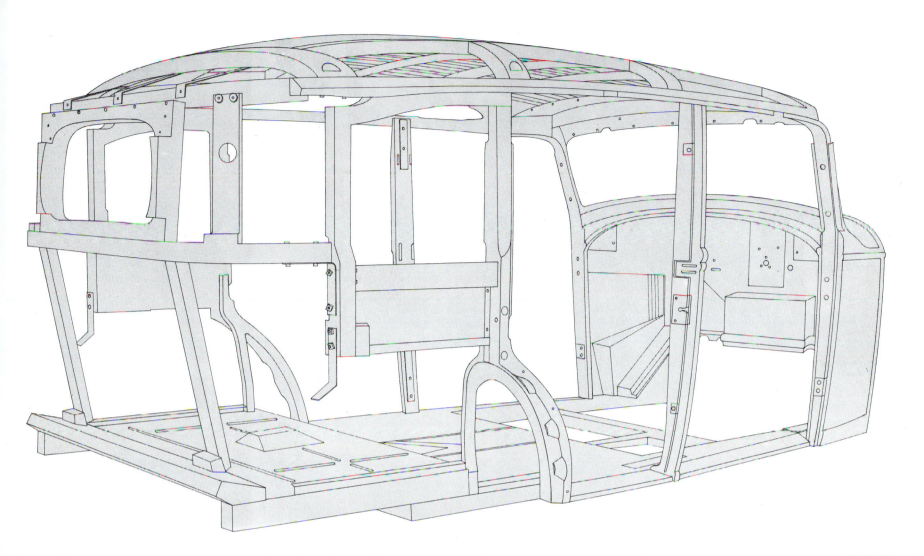

The first new stylistic theme of the thirties, the skirted-fender 1932 Graham Blue Streak (*left*). The compound curves of top and rear-quarters were not new, having been created by the Graham's designer, Amos Northup, for Reo's 1931 line. The vee-grille's rounded form, with a central bar, had first been seen on the 1929 Cord. The new fender skirts, however, were the vital touch. American manufacturers took a long, hard look at Northup's fender skirts and sloping vee-grille—and began to imitate them.

Shown (*right*) is a 1934 Ford V8, but Graham influence is also detectable on contemporary Chevrolets, Nashes, and Terraplanes, for instance. The Ford shape duplicates Graham's every way, though this three-quarter view of a Tudor Sedan shows the theme at its worst, thanks to an abbreviated wheel-base of 112 in (2.8 m) and the short hood resulting from the use of a compact vee-eight motor.

The structural picture (*top*) gives the lie to the oft-held assertion that all-metal sedan bodies were general practice in the United States throughout the 1930s. This is the framing of the 1932–33 Graham Blue Streak and is in wood, though a steel dash is used, and steel channel-selections in the forward doorposts give access to the wiring.

(*Left*) Classic shape of the early 1930s – as echoed by Chrysler, SS, and ultimately, Renault. Here is the prototype of these and many others – the L29 Cord convertible coupé as made from 1929 to 1932. Its long hood is crowned by a neat vee grille. Here a virtue was made of necessity, for the Cord's front-wheel drive called for a transmission set in front of an already lengthy straight-eight motor. This gave not only a longer hood, but also a handsome apron concealing the forward end of the drive unit. Beauty was won at the cost of indifferent forward vision. Worse, the new idiom didn't really blend with a smallish four- or six-cylinder motor, hence various stratagems had to be tried by copying makers to get proportions right. Chrysler added a vee-windshield on their 1932 line (their smaller CM of 1931 looked very stunted), while on William Lyons's SS the hood was also carried back almost as far as the windshield.

Theme and variation, or what the United States thinks today, Europe thinks tomorrow. The 1929 Chrysler line (*centre left*: this is a De Soto) popularized the ribbon radiator shell on inexpensive automobiles. The 1930 Swift from Britain (*centre right*) carefully aped it.

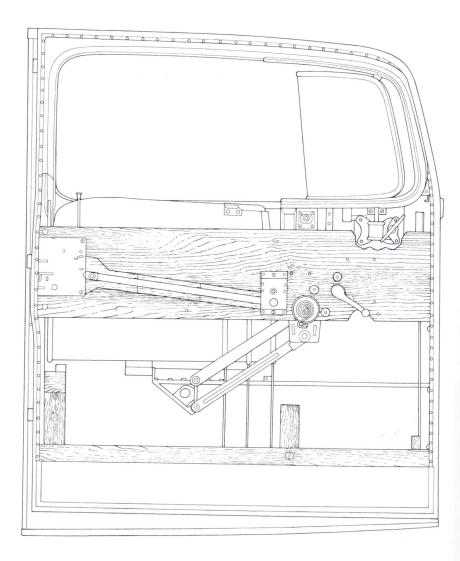

Briggs had carriage-trade connections, through their respective ownership of the Dietrich and Le Baron studios. Amos Northup, responsible for two landmarks of the 1930s, the Reo Royale and Graham's Blue Streak, was a Dietrich man. There was, however, always a good chance that a Board would turn its nose up at renderings submitted to it by mere body specialists. Nash's engineers complained that Alexis de Sakhnoffski's advanced ideas did not translate easily into sheet metal, while in order to sell his first major styling exercise to Hupmobile, the great Raymond Loewy had to buy one of their straight-eight chassis and translate it into reality at a cost to himself of $15,000 (£3,000). Nonetheless, General Motors had given the lead – and it was followed, albeit reluctantly.

In its original form, Earl's La Salle, prototype of the 1930 Cadillacs, was not a truly integrated design, though some of the Hispano-Suiza's elegance rubbed off, and it would set the fashion, in its later manifestations, for those hood doors which had become the rage in the United States by 1930; these, by the way, did not catch on wholesale in Europe, where their use was largely confined to French cars. More important, perhaps, was the narrow ribbon-type radiator shell, a more universal fad; among the shameless foreign cribs were the 1930 Fiats and Swifts.

Though La Salle influences would persist into 1931, the next phase was ushered in late in 1929 by the first Cord, largely the work of Al Leamy. Here necessity was the mother of invention: the combination of a big straight-eight motor and a frontal gearbox called for a hood of excessive length, and the whole affair was skilfully executed, with a vee grille, a shallow windshield, and a low roof-line. It is a matter of opinion whether vee windshields helped or not. Chrysler, the first of the big battalions to copy the Cord idiom, tried both configurations during the style's four-year run. Elegance was, however, won at the price of claustrophobia, and the Cord theme really needed a straight-eight to show it off to advantage. Studebaker circumvented the problem of an abbreviated six by coming up with a more aggressive vee on their 1933 and 1934 cars, but many of the smaller Chryslers looked stunted, and it is significant that the corporation never applied this style to their four-cylinder Plymouth. Everyone else, however, fell for it – even Packard, who used vee radiators from 1932 onwards. This would be just about their only concession to styling in the American sense.

The long, low look marked the first dramatic impact of American styling in Europe – La Salle themes, with their Hispano overtones, were, after all, only re-imports. The classic instance of the new idiom was, of course, William Lyons's first SS of 1932, which was pure Cord with the addition of the Old World's traditional cycle fenders, but vee radiators and long hoods also make their appearance on such conservative

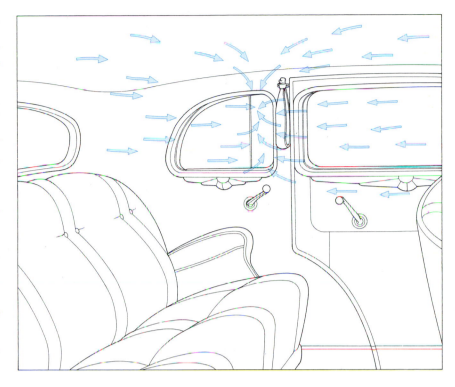

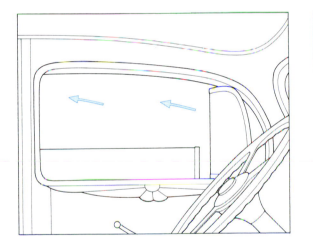

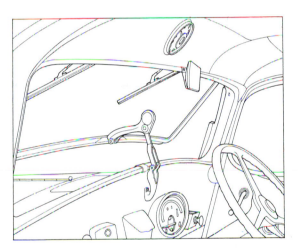

Draughtless ventilation. The Fisher system used by General Motors, showing its application to a front door (*opposite, right*), and to rear quarter-lights (*top right*). It served to complicate window-winding mechanisms more than somewhat. Further, General Motors held the patents, so other manufacturers had to figure out their own alternatives. Hudson devised an arrangement on which the ventipane at the front on the driver's side could either be wound out separately (*centre left*), or down with the main window (*centre middle*). Another Hudson feature (common to many cars on both sides of the Atlantic) was a full-opening windshield (*centre right*), a boon in fog, though presenting dust-sealing problems that would kill the idea in the end. Not that ventipanes and other sliding systems were devoid of headaches: some countries still made hand signals compulsory, and in such circumstances the arrangement was an infernal nuisance.

(*Bottom right*) The English gentleman's carriage made no concessions to styling. The Sunbeam Sixteen shape ran for six years with minimal change: one can only tell a 1931 or 1932 from a 1930 by the plated radiator shutters and hub caps, though by this time fabric bodies (Sunbeam had been prime addicts) were on their way out. Mechanically, the vehicle was refined rather than avant-garde: a pushrod six of 2.2 litres' capacity, coil ignition instead of the earlier magneto, semi-elliptic springs all round, and a four-speed transmission with right-hand shift (Sunbeam would supply a centre shift to order, but it wasn't the done thing). The accelerator pedal was, however, centrally located, and brakes were, surprisingly, hydraulic. Performance was unspectacular – about 65 mph (105 km/h) thanks to a weight of 1½ tons, but this mattered naught to the English gentleman. What did matter was his bank manager, less happy in those dark days about spending £700 ($3,500) on a mere automobile.

American shapes of the mid-thirties. The 1937 Hudson (*opposite, left*) and 1936 Studebaker (*top left*) show how others are following where General Motors led in 1934, with the compound curve. Neither is particularly successful, the Studebaker because it still uses the radiator-style grille of the Agramonte La Salle, and the Hudson because of its exaggerated waterfall arrangement out front, a mixture of Chrysler Airflow and 1935 Pontiac influences. It looked less bad with a trunkback, and Americans clearly thought so, too, though probably on grounds of the trunkback's extra baggage accommodation. (Chevrolet, who sold both shapes in 1937, unloaded over three thousand trunkbacks to every trunkless four-door sedan delivered.) The 1937 Pontiac (*top right*) is authentic General Motors, and one step further forward, mainly in the grille department, where a wide horizontal bar arrangement replaces 1936's narrow vertical band. While the make shared bodies with Oldsmobile, it was possible to distinguish the two breeds from the back as well as the front: Oldsmobile wore their tail-lamps streamlined into the body at belt level. Finally (*opposite, right*), we see a real advance, in 1938's Cadillac Sixty Special (this is actually the 1939 edition with a shorter, more attractive grille, but the rest of it is identical). Note the flowing line of the body from hood back to trunk, and the narrow European-style pillars which give an impression of light absent from the earlier turret tops. Fender treatment is tidier, too. But oh! those sidemounts! They weren't compulsory at home, but few export editions escaped the treatment.

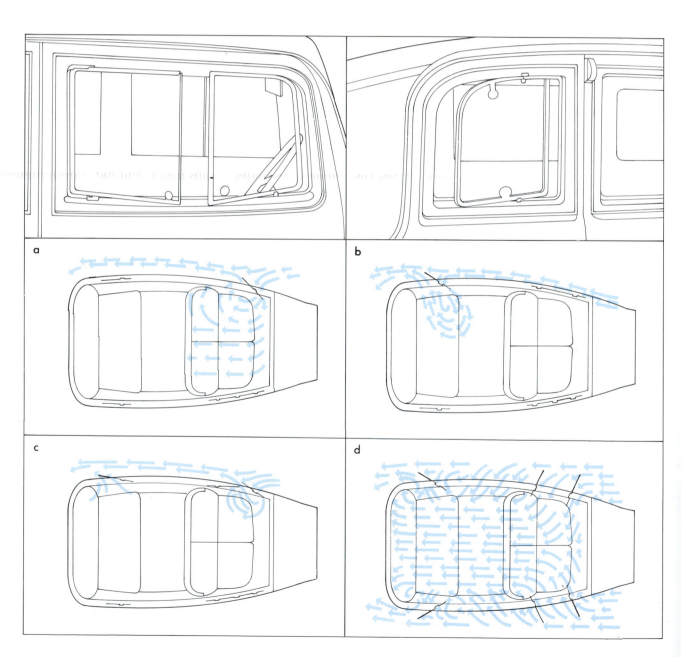

French makes as Berliet, Delaunay-Belleville, and Renault. Those who disliked the Teutonic overtones of the vee went halfway. Plated central bars sufficed on Hillmans and Standards; Citroën's 1933 models added a gentle curve, accentuated by some more chromium plating, already the stylist's best friend. The Germans and Czechs, already addicted to the vee motif, fell wholesale for long hoods, the ultimate, perhaps, being achieved on Busek's 1934 Aero, a 1-litre twin with, admittedly, front-wheel drive.

Having achieved a motif, the stylists now set to work to tidy the automobile up. The first major victim was the sedan's unsightly projecting forepeak. This was cured by a surfeit of compound curves; at the same time, fenders were given skirts. This fashion was ushered in on Northup's 1931 Reo Royale, though the celebrated skirts did not appear until a year later on the same designer's Graham, immortalized in the nurseries of the world by the Tootsie Toy company. The Graham also jettisoned hood doors in favour of inclined louvres, and everyone else followed suit, patterns of plated "speed streaks" being all the vogue. Graham influence was immediately detectable on the mid-1932 efforts of a desperate Willys-Overland Motors, on the 1933 Ford V8, and, as a clumsy parody, on Nash's 1934 line. Ford exported it to Europe on

their first true "foreign" car, the 933-cc Model Y made by Dagenham and Cologne alike, though they spoilt the effect by omitting fender skirts from the first series. These were hurriedly added towards the end of 1933.

Not that the excrescences had gone, by any means. Radiator filler caps might, and did, vanish underhood, even if such traditional European mascots as Mercedes' three-pointed star and Armstrong Siddeley's sphinx would remain functional for some years to come. But headlamps still lived out of doors, fenders stayed separate, and those handsome if not very practical sidemounts were still with us (try hauling a 19-inch wheel out of one of those rust traps on a wet day!). Trunks of any kind were confined to accessory catalogues. The big gimmick of 1933 from General Motors was Fisher No-Draft Ventilation: small ventipanes in the front windows which admitted air in controlled amounts. By 1935, the rest of the industry had similar ideas, but in the meantime, Harley Earl and Jules Agramonte had come up with the new straight-eight La Salle.

Here the designers were looking skywards, and aeronautical themes were predominant. Headlamps were now attached to the radiator grille (Rover had had a similar line in 1914). The compound curve had

Draughtless ventilation by numbers, or Packard's explanation of their new 1934 controlled system (*opposite*). It looks unnecessarily complicated, and it is – General Motor's Fisher No-Draft Ventilation was simpler, but it was also heavily patented, hence it was more important to avoid infringement suits than it was to be logical. Reading clockwise, the four lower diagrams show how air-flow is directed where passengers want it. (*a*) indicates front-seat ventilation regulated by the forward sections in the front windows. (*b*)

shows the way the rear quarter windows limit air supply to the back seats when used alone. In (*c*) all the quarter windows are open for the convenience of smokers on a wet day (cigarettes were not yet a dirty word), while (*d*) gives us air-flow unlimited on a stewing midwestern summer day. Not shown is an "impression of chaos" in which conventional windows are proved to direct all the air down the passengers' necks! The top two pictures show the actual mechanics of the system. Packard favoured a split arrangement, though

everything at least opened in the same plane if not in the same direction. In front (*left*) there was a vertical split, though whether this helped "quick signalling" is open to question: those who have driven 1960s Minis in countries where hand signals are still compulsory would doubtless confirm that there's no substitute for a traditional wind-down window. Nobody, fortunately, had patented the orthodox-opening rear quarter-light (*right*), which was definitely an improvement on a wind-down arrangement. Either type, though

common enough in the United States, was regarded as a luxury in Europe, and they were always a problem, the Packard type emitting a distasteful whistle at high speeds. One of the blessings we owe (indirectly) to the Cadillac Sixty Special and its stylists is the ultimate abandonment of the six-light (three-window, to Americans) principle in sedan bodies. Ventilation headaches apart, this meant fewer pillars and better vision once the wrap-round rear window had been achieved.

The straight-eight La Salle (*bottom*) was the style leader of its era, though by the time this 1935 example was made, the design was a year old, and its influence could be detected in Studebakers and Hudsons as well as in the rest of the General Motors range. Also it had lost its original biplane bumpers, too expensive even for the upper-middle-class market. Most significant, perhaps, were the "turret top" body with its compound curves, the pontoon fenders, and the retreat of the radiator. If this vogue for the tall and narrow didn't last long, grilles contracted in other directions. Other integrating touches were the attachment of the headlamps to the grille, and the disappearance underhood of the radiator filler cap. The "disc" wheels were, of course, only fancy covers concealing the steel-spoke type (as on English Talbots and Sunbeam-Talbots a few years later), while the portholes on the hood would reappear as a Buick hallmark in 1949, long after the La Salle's demise. On the mechanical side, the La Salle was General Motors's first car with hydraulic brakes, the coil-spring independent front suspension was found also on 1934 Cadillacs (and in a different form on lesser General Motors models as well), and the mechanics were basically Oldsmobile Eight, though owners soon discovered that there was little parts-interchange-ability between the two breeds. At $1,650 (£330) for a sedan in 1934, however, the new car kept the wheels turning at Cadillac Division: of 13,014 cars delivered that season, more than half were the inexpensive straight-eights.

Integration taken a step further – on the 1941 Chevrolet sedan (*top right*). Mechanically, it is still the good old splash-lubricated 3.5-litre six-cylinder Cast Iron Wonder, but running boards have gone, headlamps have retreated into the fenders, and the new alligator hood permits shallower grilles which make up in width for what they've lost in height. Fenders and bumpers are gradually becoming part of a whole, if not necessarily a very harmonious one. The United States, of course, was not yet at war, and inflation had not bitten, so Chevrolet's cheapest four-door sedan cost only $795 (£159); "special de luxe" equipment added only another $56 (£10.20). Curiously, at the bottom of the market two-door sedans still outsold the four-door type (safer with young children?). What did one get on the world's best-selling automobile? Ninety hp, 80–85 mph (130–135 km/h), and cheap flat-rate servicing throughout the United States. Over 900,000 Americans thought the Chevrolet was a good buy in the last year of peace.

progressed a step further with the curvaceous metal Turret Top; it drummed infuriatingly, especially since Americans, unlike Britons, would have no truck with the sliding roof. The latest pontoon fenders were reminiscent of the then-fashionable aircraft-wheel spats, and even the bumpers were of "biplane" type. (The bumpers cost too much, so they were axed after one year.) Trunks were now integral and projected rearwards to give adequate baggage accommodation with external access. The radiator grille was tall and narrow, and once again, a spate of copies ensued. La Salle influences were detectable on the 1935 models of Hudson and Studebaker.

Alas! some untidying processes were also at work. After 1935, only Packard and the dying house of Pierce-Arrow sported grilles with any resemblance to the traditional radiator, while chromium plate came into its own. The prevailing theme of 1936 was the fencer's mask, seen at its worst on the Hudson, the Pontiac, and the curious Triumph Dolomite in England. This one was especially horrible, since the new masterpiece of die-casting was flanked by all the traditional British paraphernalia – separate fenders and headlamps, spotlamps, and twin wind-tone horns, another American import soon to be banished indoors by the march of integration. Horizontal bars replaced the fencing theme in 1937 and 1938, but in the meantime, Cadillac had taken a step forward with the Sixty Special.

The original grille of the Sixty Special was abominable, but the rest of it, if not wholly European in concept, achieved an excellent balance, with recessed running boards, a trunk which blended perfectly with the body lines and no longer resembled a gratuitous afterthought, and headlamps partially faired into the front fenders. The European four-window configuration with its thin pillars dispelled the claustrophobic air characteristic of American designs since the days of the L29 Cord. All General Motors makes had four-window notchbacks available by 1941. So had Studebaker, though Chrysler's Town Sedans remained fastbacks, and for several years, the industry hedged its bets between these two idioms.

Retreat into convention, or Chrysler's headline-making teardrop-shaped Airflow of 1934 (*lower*) was too much for Americans. This one was a straight-eight, though you could also have a 4-litre six with De Soto badges. The cars were tricky to maintain and pitched badly. The latter ailment was never fully cured, but by 1936, in an attempt to render looks more attractive, Chrysler had tacked on this curious widow's-peak grille. They also added a projecting trunk at the rear, which gave external luggage access at the price of inferior aerodynamics and a less balanced appearance. The last straw was the aggressive grille (very similar to that of regular Chryslers) used in 1937; less than 5,000 of the season's 108,000 new cars were Airflows, and they were to be the last. Henceforward, orthodoxy was the order of the day, as witness this 1939 C23 Imperial (*top*) using the same 5.3-litre engine as the old Airflow. Some Airflow influence survives in the fastback sedan body (favoured also by Ford, though General Motors preferred trunkbacks). In other respects, the car does not differ strongly from its rivals: alligator hood, receding grille and running boards, recessed headlamps, and column shift, plus the independent front suspension that the corporation had tried unsuccessfully in 1934, though never on Airflows.

Buick

The Doctor's Friend, 1936 style. In fact, the Buick Special's one cardinal feature, the overhead-valve straight-eight engine, is not shown at all. On the chassis (*bottom right*), one notes some characteristic 1936 items: the rigid cruciform bracing of the frame (*a*), the coil-spring independent front suspension of short- and long-arm type (*b*), the 16-in (40.6 cm) wheels and low-pressure tyres (*c*), and the hydraulic brakes (*d*), these last rapidly becoming the rule in the United States, though Ford would hold out with mechanicals for another three seasons. The complete car demonstrates to what extent the cult of the compound curve was carried. There is not a single sharp angle in sight. Vee windshields and large integral trunks were new on Buicks that year, though

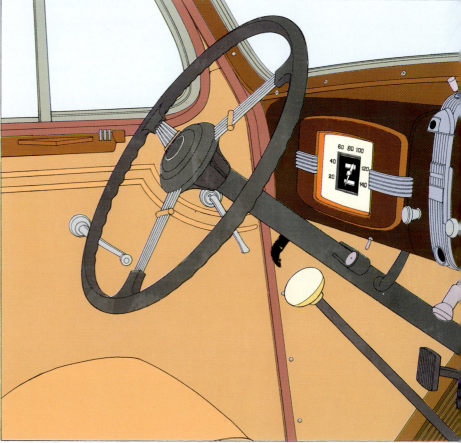

they'd already been seen on other General Motors cars in 1935. The steel-spoke wheels had only a year more to run: full discs would be in fashion by 1937. Headlamps and running boards are still exposed, and front fenders sufficiently unstreamlined to cope with the dual sidemounts. The trunk (*bottom left*) suggests that fitted suitcases were standard, which they were not, though when un-cluttered by a spare wheel it could almost have accommodated the "two sturdy teenagers and a Great Dane" cited in Buick's catalogues. Within the "office" (*bottom centre*), styling triumphs over all other considerations. Even the clock on the glovebox lid matches the integrated but not very legible "information display" in front of the driver. The vee windshield was not an aid to forward vision, while the gearshift still sits firmly on the floor; note that as on most American cars of the period, it is cranked slightly forward to allow of three people on the front seat. And on the far left under the dash is yet another umbrella-handle handbrake.

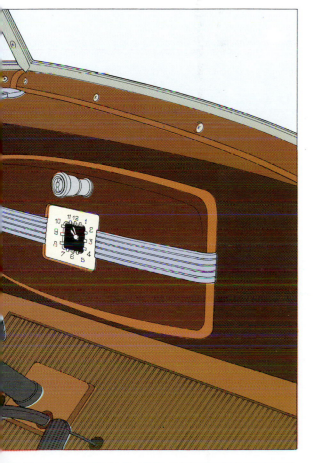

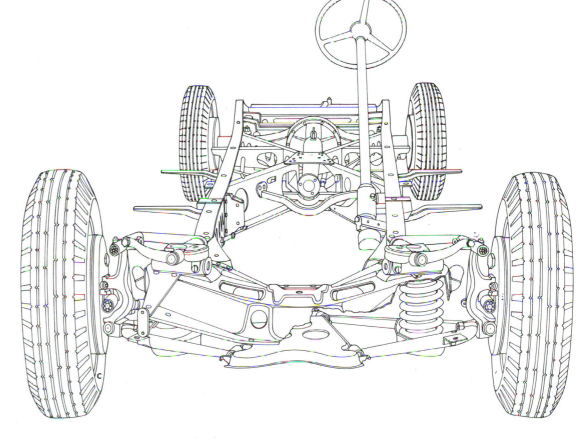

Facias various. Styled panels were not only American. A very odd one is found on the 1935 Singer Nine sports coupé (*bottom right*). In an attempt to avoid glare, the facia, otherwise conventional, is mounted at an acute angle.

The visual horror of the American idiom is detectable in the 1938 Lincoln Zephyr (*opposite, top left*), though the central dial is easy to read, adaptable to left- or right-hand steering, and allows plenty of room for radio and locker. By contrast, the 1938 British SS 100 shows a typical sports car layout, with big speedometer and rev counter in front of the driver. The other instruments are somewhat haphazardly disposed. The folding windshield is typical of the 1930s sports car, and on the SS there are also miniature aero screens to protect the crew when the main windshield is lowered. On the 1939 2.6-litre WA-type MG (*opposite, bottom*) the manufacturer's traditional octagon motif is perpetuated in the shape of the dials. Ergonomic influences are visible in the neatly grouped switches below the facia, though starter and ignition switches are separate.

Sheer glamour, a checkered production history, and technical problems connected with the front-wheel drive and electric gear shift tend to detract from the stylistic merits of the 1936 810 Cord, here seen (*left*) in its most sought-after form, the 1937 812-series supercharged phaeton

Further strides were made after Europe went to war. The glass industry, admittedly, had yet to master the single-panel curved screen, albeit Chrysler had used one on their biggest Airflows, and Hupmobile's Aerodynamic featured wrap-round inserts in the windshield posts. Gradually, however, grille, front fenders, and bumpers merged into dissonances of aggressive chromium plate, fuel fillers were flush-mounted, and rear fenders were integrated into the body. Cars grew steadily longer, Pontiacs gaining sixteen inches between 1936 and 1942.

Not all the clever ideas caught on. One that fortunately failed was the Chrysler Airflow, with its flush sides, spatted rear wheels, and waterfall grille. It found no native imitators, albeit direct cribs were perpetrated by Singer in Britain, Volvo in Sweden, and Toyota in Japan. But though stylists were becoming adept at selling their masterpieces to the public, the Airflow was altogether too much. Its alligator hood, with high, flush sides, made maintenance awkward, and early cars had no external luggage access. Neither Britons nor Swedes wanted it either: the Volvo Carioca sold poorly, while most of the 11-hp Singer chassis earmarked for the new idiom were completed with conventional bodies. Even when hurriedly reworked, first with a new widow's-peak grille and then with a bigger trunk, the Airflow proved a lemon. Another one that backfired was the 1932 Hupmobile with Loewy's cycle fenders: it coincided with the skirted Graham, and the dressier car appealed more.

Regrettably disregarded – or, more correctly, bowdlerized – was Gordon Buehrig's 810 Cord, the sensation of 1936. If the manually retractable headlamps were a gimmick and before their time, the low-mounted, wrap-round grille was an excellent idea. But where Buehrig's original was simple and unadorned, his would-be imitators laid the chromium on with a trowel. One has only to study the Chrysler Corporation's 1939 range to see what went wrong, though one cannot but admire the skill with which bar-patterns were cunningly shuffled to give four different front-end treatments for the four makes in the group.

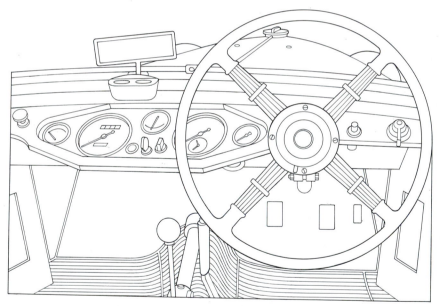

(four-passenger convertible coupé). This one was good for over 100 mph (160 km/h) on 4.7 litres and 190 bhp. Gordon Buehrig's creation had an elegant simplicity of line, with the unadorned horizontal bars of the grille extending round on to the sides of the alligator-type hood. There was no superfluous chromium plate, and the radiator core was completely hidden. Also streamlined in was the fuel filler cap, while running boards were dispensed with, and the headlamps (here seen fully extended for use) were fully retractable, though they had to be wound in and out by hand. A curved front apron concealed the drive units: this

was, of course, a legacy from the original 1929 Cord.

Unsuccessful mimicry. Sweden's imitation of the 1934 Chrysler Airflow, the Volvo PV36 Carioca (*opposite, top right*). The fast back, rear fender skirts, divided windshield, and raised hood sides incorporating nacelles for the recessed headlamps are authentic Chrysler, though Volvo eschewed Chrysler's original 1934 waterfall grille in favour of their own version of the later "widow's peak". Unfortunately, the Swedes disliked the shape just as the Americans had, and precisely five hundred Cariocas found buyers.

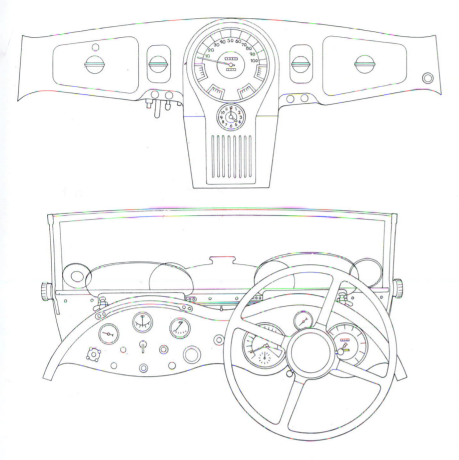

"What Detroit thinks today, Europe thinks tomorrow", though the Auto Union group in Saxony were pretty quick off the mark in this particular car. The front end of their Wanderer W24 reflects the 1937 General Motors idiom announced in the fall of 1936, and the German car was first seen at Berlin the following March. What one can see here (*centre*), however, shows that Auto Union had adopted the American idiom for the first time, though it was as yet limited to this Wanderer and the four-cylinder DKW with very similar chassis and sheet metal. The curved and skirted fenders, vestigial running boards,

and ventipanes in the front windows are purest Detroit, as are the smooth flow of the roof-line and the fully integrated rear trunk, even if the spare wheel lives out of doors in the interests of *Lebensraum*, and luggage is accessible only from inside. Technically, of course, Germany is ahead of the United States. Though Wanderer are content with a stolid four-cylinder side-valve motor giving 42 bhp from 1.8 litres and propelling the car at an equally staid 65 mph (105 km/h), all four wheels are independently sprung and brakes are hydraulic, at a time when Ford, at any rate, were still wedded to mechanicals.

Second-hand American ideas. Only the fencer's mask grilles link the 1939 Rosengart LR4 (*bottom*) and the 1936 Riley Sprite (*opposite*). Motives were different, too. The French firm was trying to update its version of the Austin Seven, by this time blessed with conventional suspension and a more robust frame. The result was certainly chic, but rumour said that this cabriolet cost more than the imported British article, for all the swingeing tariffs, and sales of 5,650 cars in 1939 were hardly impressive. The Riley's grille was peculiar to this model and concealed the regular radiator. Power was provided by Riley's excellent twin-camshaft high-pushrod 1,496-cc four in twin-carburettor form, and the Sprite would do 85 mph (135–140 km/h). The works raced them (with light bodies and no fancy trimmings) and won both the 1935 and 1936 Tourist Trophies. With those big exposed headlamps and heavy fenders, one may doubt if the grille made much difference to the aerodynamics: many owners threw them away.

The stylist's brief, of course, did not end outside an automobile. He went to work on the inside, with interesting and sometimes curious consequences to the facia.

Dashboards themselves were a concomitant of the new streamlined facias of 1914–15. In the early 1920s, instruments were dotted haphazardly all over the place, though central groupings were becoming accepted practice by 1927, if not earlier. Further, they tended to be of postage-stamp size, while in the ascendant was one of the nastier American innovations, the drum-type speedometer on which only the actual speed of the moment was exposed to view. Such a device was standard even on the lordly Model-J Duesenberg, introduced in 1929.

Stylized panels soon appeared. The air-cooled Franklin featured vertical dials of unpleasing aspect, and those of the 1934 and 1935 SSs

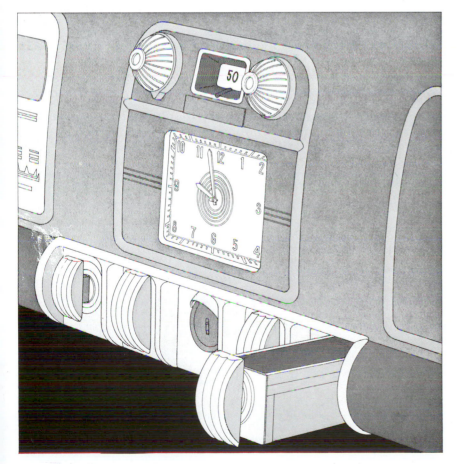

Pontiac facia (left), 1938. On this picture, the main dial can't be seen, but neatly styled into the secondary grouping are the radio (no push-button tuning as yet) and clock. Though Pontiac didn't follow some other makes in duplicating the radiator grille on the ashtray lid, the famous Silver Streaks are there for all to see!

were hexagonal, in answer to MG's well-established octagon, mercifully banished at almost all times from the facia. Thereafter, no holds were barred, horrors including Hudsons's curved panel of 1936 (to match the compound curves outdoors) and the unattractive rectangular display of 1939 Buicks. Sometimes, the nonsense was carried to extremes: the lids of Buick's 1936 ashtrays were miniature replicas of the radiator grille.

There were some compensations. In the main, instruments were now grouped where the driver could see them, and simplicity was the order of the day. The redeeming feature of the single oval dial on 1936 Hillmans was a huge ignition warning-light, the size of a bantam's egg, and tailor-made for the absent-minded housewife. Less commendable was an increasing tendency to replace instruments by warning lights, not always colour-coded in those days. Mercifully, nobody had yet anticipated Nash's 1949 brainstorm: on their Airflyte series all the instruments were grouped in a single binnacle attached to the steering column. Quite apart from problems of focussing, there was a miniature

German themes, 1938–39. One expects some similarities between the 1939 Opel Kapitän (*top left*) and the 1938 Oldsmobiles on the opposite page – both makes come, after all, from General Motors. The newer Opel goes one step further, not so much with the grille but with the fully recessed headlamps. The cabriolet body and its flashy two-toning are the coachbuilder's doing; not so the fenders extending back into the doors, which are found also on the fully unitary sedan examples of this 2.4-litre overhead-valve six. Germans, of course, expected a full cabriolet in the range, which made it worth Opel's while to offer a separate chassis version even of a mass-produced car.

The aerodynamic 2.5-litre Adler (*bottom*) was a more expensive contemporary of the Opel, listing at a price some forty-five per cent higher in sedan form. Despite the suggestion of this drawing, it wasn't a unitary hull, being based on a punt-shaped chassis frame with heavy box-section side members, not unlike that found on Adler's smaller front-wheel-

drive cars. The rest of the top-hamper, including fenders, was delivered from the Ambi-Budd bodyworks in Berlin and then mounted on the chassis. As befits an *Autobahn*-cruiser, spotlamps as well as headlamps were fully recessed, though legal requirements in some countries dictated that the parking lights stayed out of doors. One of the disadvantages of the

perfect teardrop shape was a marked lack of rearward vision.

"We only export last year's styling themes", or this looks like a page of '38s from America. Actually, only the two Oldsmobiles (*opposite, bottom*) are from that model year; the Berliet Dauphine sedan (*opposite, top*) was the Lyonnais company's

new model for 1939, this in spite of the more conservative, fully exposed headlamps. One may suspect that this may have been a deliberate attempt to conceal the origins of the Berliet's body, bought complete from Peugeot of Sochaux and common to that company's 2.1-litre 402. (Peugeot, of course, tucked *their* headlamps *inside* the radiator grille.) The

THE MOST SUCCESSFUL
PRODUCT OF GENERAL MOTORS

OLDSMOBILE
Six and Eight

Oldsmobiles epitomize the themes of 1938: partly recessed illuminations, disappearing running boards, bumper overriders, and grilles composed of an assortment of horizontal bars. Oldsmobile's outer shell had a distinctive shape (it cropped up in unlikely places on motifs all over the car), while a neat trick was the use of a finer grille pattern to distinguish the more expensive straight-eight (*right*) from the six (*left*). This method of differentiation was on its way out: by the time the United States went to war, the big variation would be between trunkbacks and fastbacks (under sundry appellations), and one relied on hood length (or badging) to tell whether the car was a six or an eight.

forest of electrical spaghetti sharing the column with the gear-lever linkage!

Predictably, most of these American influences crossed the Atlantic, though styling was far more haphazard there, and too many popular models, especially French ones, resembled obsolete American sedans. Early examples of the integral trunk were far from practical. The French, who had long been addicted to *conduites intérieures avec malle*, kept their trunk, still opening from the top and seldom integrated into the body line. The British tendency was to add a nicely integrated excrescence at the rear and then fill it with the spare wheel, thus defeating the entire object. Fastbacks, too, were tried, though they had a short vogue, owing to limitations of rear-seat headroom. Morris and Standard were back with notchbacks by 1939, though Hillman's gentler slope was only sacrificed in favour of bigger trunks on the 1940 line. Fiat and Peugeot used the fencer's-mask idiom to good purpose: the short beetling hoods were unsightly but gave excellent forward vision, even if the French maker's trick of tucking the headlamps inside the grille was scarcely a bright idea. On the 1939 Morris 8, the headlamps vanished into the front fenders.

Even those big cars innocent of direct American antecedents looked curiously American. The Oldsmobile-like grille of the last pre-war Berliets was not improved by Marius Berliet's frugal practice of using Peugeot bodies; the Renault combined all the worst aspects of the Detroit idiom; and the 1940 Austins looked like scaled-down 1938 General Motors products – Austin would not catch up with the 1940 idiom for another seven years. In Sweden, Volvo tried a bit of everything: after the Airflow-inspired Carioca came the PV 51/52, a mixture of Chrysler and Chevrolet. Successive sixes spanning the war years incorporated the 1938 American Ford grille, the same breed's 1942 box fenders, and finally (in the post-war PV60), a Dodge-style body wedded to a 1939 Pontiac front end.

The styling revolution, of course, played its part in harassing the weaker brethren, already hard put to it to stay the course. In addition to keeping their product competitive, they had to make it look up-to-date. To mechanical gimmicks had to be added styling oddities. Graham, who had run out of cash and new ideas alike after exploring centrifugal blowers, tried an astonishing and shark-like concave nose in 1938, before joining forces with Hupmobile to exploit the body dies of the now-defunct Cord. It availed them not at all. In the same class fall Singer's curious "Airstream" experiments and Triumph's Hudson-*cum*-Pontiac front end.

The effect was felt worst in France, where the local Big Three were fast approaching the pre-eminence of General Motors, Ford, and Chrysler on the far shore of the Atlantic. Scissors and paste were now the order of the day. You either made your own chassis and bought bodies, or cloaked someone else's mechanics in a style that camouflaged their origins. Berliet bought bodies from Peugeot, and La Licorne from Citroën; cheaper Delahayes were seen with both Citroën and Renault sedan coachwork. Rosengart and Georges Irat created sporty (if not overly sporting) models from the proven mechanical elements of the 11CV Citroën *traction*. Chenard-Walcker, already humiliated by having to share bodies with Matford, were down by the outbreak of war to a choice between a Ford-bodied Citroën and a Ford-bodied Ford, though at least their suspensions came from the all-French source. Badge-engineering was upon us.

Not that this was new. A choice of radiator grille, sentiment, and customer ignorance could produce two identities out of one design. If Morris-Wolseley permutations were not as yet wholly rationalized, the goings-on at Coventry's respected Daimler factory were confusing in the extreme. At the height of their badge-engineering phase, in 1935, it

Contrasting coupés, 1938–39. The 2-litre Dolomite Roadster Coupé with six-cylinder pushrod motor (*top left*) was the flagship of the ailing Triumph company, and, unusually for a British convertible, featured a rumble seat at the rear. It looks a little naked without the accessory wheel discs usually fitted, and it's a matter of opinion whether that fancy die-cast grille in the 1936 Hudson or Pontiac idiom really blends with a traditional British shape. Still, it was good for 85–90 mph (135–145 km/h) and won rallies as well as *concours d'elégance*. By contrast, one expects a rumble seat on the 1938 Dodge (*bottom left*), though this style was also available as a Business Coupé with baggage space instead of extra seating. This British-assembled car has a plethora of extra illumination. There's a rumble seat again on the rare front-wheel-drive Citroën *faux cabriolet* (*bottom right*), offered only from 1934 to 1938, though the solid steel top and fixed rear window made the extra passengers feel "quarantined". This 1938 7CV is the British model with 12-volt electrics and leather trim. By contrast, the foursome drophead coupé (convertible victoria) was essentially a European type as late as 1938, when this semi-custom Vauxhall 14/6 (*top right*) by Salmons-Tickford was built, almost the last of its line, since 1939 Fourteens were unitary and available only as sedans. Sold through Vauxhall's own dealer chain, the car featured a three-position top, the usual claustrophobic rear quarters, and the never very satisfactory arrangement of a spare wheel mounted on the trunk lid.

was hard to sort out the various Tens and Light Sixes produced under the BSA and Lanchester banners, while only a name, a radiator, and £20 ($100), distinguished the Lanchester Eighteen from the Daimler Light Twenty. Both were 2.6-litre overhead-valve sixes rated at 20 hp under the British fiscal system.

Beneath even the most doleful 1930s shapes, however, could be discerned a new aspect of the automobile – a living room on wheels. This was, after all, only logical. The vehicle already offered dependable transportation, and the stylists had integrated its lines. Now, it was time to make it truly habitable.

The writer can recall long winter journeys in the 1930s, mainly in mass-produced British sedans. The entire crew dressed up in overcoats, and rear-seat passengers were armed with hot-water bottles. At least one window was open. Not, be it said, for hand signals – semaphore-type turn indicators had reached Germany by the late 1920s and the rest of Europe by 1934 – but to prevent the glass from frosting up. Wise motorists carried a raw potato to scrape frost from the windshield itself, since the accessory bar demisters of the period were less than efficient. Seats adjusted but did not recline, and though the average British car of 1935 was well equipped – the mandatory sliding roof, a remotely controlled rear blind, leather upholstery, arm-rests, an opening windshield, and even a clock – there was no heater.

By this time, such an amenity was a regular optional extra in the United States. Nash scored a bullseye in 1938 with their "air-conditioning", though in fact this was only a controlled heating and ventilation system. Real air-conditioning would not arrive until 1941, on the more expensive Packards. The windshield washer, essential if not compulsory in most countries today, was in its infancy. True, such a device was found on some 1935 Standards and Triumphs, but since it used radiator water, its early demise was predictable. More sophisticated versions were available in the United States by 1938. Bed-seats, pioneered by Durant in 1931, reappeared seven years later on Nash's extras list, while power assistance was being applied to the divider windows of limousines as well as to the tops of convertibles.

There was also the question of in-car entertainment. Car radio was one of the major amenities of 1930s motoring. Admittedly, reception was not up to modern standards, for all such eccentricities as "streetcar" settings on early American installations. Antennae were a constant problem, with whip-shaped circlets on the roof, and even an under-the-running-board type, recommended only for use on ragtops.

Progress was slow at first. Though several American manufacturers advertized their cars as "wired for radio" in 1931, factory installation was not part of the programme, since the work could take two competent technicians a good eight hours to complete. In spite of these early complications, Americans bought 145,000 car radios in 1932, and over a million in 1935. By this time, too, dashboards were being tailored to accept radio panels, which often meant scrapping a few automobile-oriented dials in favour of "idiot lights". Push-button tuning was a reality by 1939, and a vacuum-powered antenna was actually a catalogued option on 1940 Pontiacs.

The tempo was slower in Europe. Hillman's 1934 Melody Minx was one of the first cars offered with "factory radio", but on most conversions the control panel lived under the dash, where it barked the front-seat passenger's knees. The same improvisation went for heaters, where fitted; the fan on the writer's 1937 MG was positioned strategically within inches of his clutch foot, so that a fast downshift would produce sepulchral clanks from this unit. It was not until 1939 that the first built-in installations appeared on popular cars. By this time, music while one drove was quite cheap: SS Cars quoted a mere £20 ($100) inclusive of fitting, on their last pre-war models.

In the United States the drawing-room image went much further. Thanks to the Japanese, only fifteen thousand Pontiacs were sold in 1942, but the "personalization" available to customers went far beyond the nine single-tone and five two-tone colour choices. Far, indeed, beyond five different choices of cloth trim and the practical option of a booster for those inefficient vacuum wipers still beloved of Americans. Seat covers came in nine patterns, there was a "Kool Kushion" for long spells at the wheel, and the presence of an "in-car bed" showed that General Motors had no intention of losing out to Nash. "Vizor vanity mirrors" came with or without illumination, an extra ashtray could be attached to the front ventipane, and lights could be installed in the trunk and glove compartments. Entertainment was not limited to the in-car variety: Pontiac Division could sell you a portable radio for picnics. And if, in this aura of "thermostatic heat" and "controlled no-draft ventilation", you caught a cold, your friendly dealer was ready with a Kleenex dispenser to clip under the dash.

4

CRYING ONE'S WARES

Automotive publicity went to town in the 1930s.

True, it was not as yet internationally oriented. Car exports still meant the United States first and foremost. Detroit's offerings might be gaining in bulk, sophistication, and ballyhoo, but they still enjoyed the widest distribution, just as they had in the 1920s, and, indeed, during most of the teens.

Unquestionably, Henry Ford's successful pursuit of mass production had been the main ingredient of this American dominance, but it was the First World War that opened the floodgates. All the other major car-making nations were now preoccupied with weightier matters. Even if a "business as usual" philosophy – plus a marked inefficiency in conversion to the weapons of war – allowed Britan's motor industry to turn out a fair number of passenger cars in 1915 and 1916, there were not enough to go round. Thus, American-built automobiles by the thousand suddenly invaded not only England, but also Britain's still-numerous dominions and colonies. Here their continuing hegemony was assured by low prices, ease of maintenance, and characteristics better suited to bush roads than anything offered by the rest of Europe.

Italy, of course, imported nothing, while German interest in American cars was a phenomenon of the later 1920s. France, however, proved fertile soil for Ford, if not for his up-market rivals; the government alone took eleven thousand new Ts and TT trucks in 1918, thus paving the way for the establishment of an assembly plant in Bordeaux soon after the Armistice.

Thenceforward, the United States moved in with a vengeance. During the 1930s, General Motors were assembling in Belgium, Germany, and Great Britain, not to mention in Australia and Japan. Ford operations were on a similar scale, while the youthful Chrysler Corporation were never far behind. The relaxation of Belgian tariff barriers in the 1920s not only administered the *coup de grâce* to that country's automobile industry, it opened the way for Antwerp's assembly plants.

Nor was this the limit. South America might be short on roads – even Argentina, her wealthiest republic, still had no all-weather system linking all her major cities – but this was no deterrent to Detroit. Ford, who began operations there in 1922, merely shipped carloads of Ts to the nearest convenient railhead. General Motors were assembling Chevrolets in the country by 1927, and Julio Fevre, the Chrysler concessionaire in Buenos Aires, was in the assembly business as well five years later.

The Great Depression was to take its toll. Even where prices were competitive – and they usually were – a Buick used more fuel than an Austin or Citroën. It also carried a higher annual tax. This, however, bit only where the impost was directly related to cylinder capacity or fuel consumption, as in Britain or France. In the former country American sales took a tumble in the 1930–32 period, and breeds as well-known and respected as Cadillac, Dodge, Nash, Studebaker, and even Chevrolet disappeared from the market. Nations with industries to protect protected them savagely; with the accession of Hitler, Germany, which had taken twenty-two thousand vehicles from General Motors alone in 1928, became virtually a closed shop. Czechoslovak duties inflated the list price of a Ford V8 – $500 (£100) at home and $1,300 (£260) in Britain – to an uneconomic $4,000 (£800). Even Switzerland adopted a protectionist policy, though she was locking the stable door after the horse had bolted. Martini, her sole passenger-car maker, was moribund in 1928 and dead by 1934.

Elsewhere Detroit ruled the roost. Even in 1933, the American automotive industry exported 63,754 cars – only four per cent of total production, but then the still-substantial demand for right-hand steering was filled from Canadian plants. Canada shipped twenty-nine per cent of her output abroad that year, the percentage reaching thirty-three in 1936, and again in 1938. We shall return to the realm of exports later on; suffice it to say for the moment that only American or American-owned concerns thought globally in their public relations.

This factor would govern the crying of wares. Only in specialist cases was advertising directed at a specific overseas market: in 1937, Chevrolet spent a lot of money promoting their new Cheetah model, with a taxable horsepower of only twenty-five, a good bet (or so they hoped) in Britain, where the regular G-series was rated as a thirty. Otherwise, export advertising consisted quite simply of fitting translated copy round a layout already tried out on the domestic market. (For right-hand drive one reversed the block!) Thus, we find Essex inflicting some truly American publicity on Swedes in 1930. "A Car for the Whole Family", proclaimed the copy-writer. "The Essex is not just a car for yourself, but for your whole family, because it is roomy – roomier than before, and roomier than other cars of the same size. You can easily get in and out through the extra-wide doors, you sit comfortably, and the car is comfortable and easy to drive." To make certain that Swedes (not to mention Brazilians and Britons) knew that it really was "roomier than before", a suitably distorted line block rather than a photograph accompanied this outburst. It made the boxy Essex look twenty feet long, and it got to Stockholm way ahead of the actual car.

Slogans, of course, didn't always translate. Hotchkiss's *le juste milieu* sounded fine in French, but "the golden mean" (not used in English-speaking countries) suggested too much compromise. Daimler, wisely,

...DÈS LES PREMIERS BEAUX JOURS PAR MONTS ET PAR VAUX AU VOLANT D'UNE

9 cv 4 cyl 4 vit OU 11 cv 4 cyl 4 vit

BERLIET

SANS SOUCIS, AVEC UN MINIMUM DE SOINS VOUS AUREZ TOUJOURS LA PLUS GRANDE SATISFACTION. REMARQUÉS PAR VOTRE ÉLÉGANCE, ENVIÉS POUR VOTRE CONFORT, VOUS APPRÉCIEREZ **LES SOUPAPES EN TÊTE ET LES 4 VITESSES : DEUX FACTEURS D'ÉCONOMIE.**

USINES ET BUREAUX, VÉNISSIEUX (RHONE)

BOULEVARD DE VERDUN, COURBEVOIE (SEINE)

How to add charm to utility. If one had to pick two of the most mundane cars of the 1930s, the Model A Ford (here in English guise) and the 1934 four-cylinder Berliet from France would be "naturals". Actually, the Ford, with a gearshift compared to "slicing butter with a hot knife", was not without a certain charm, and anything would have been a welcome change after the idiosyncracies of Model T. Since, at £225 ($1,125) ex-works Manchester, the car was considerably more expensive than the native Morris-Cowley, Ford of Britain were stressing the up-market, miniature Lincoln image with real photographs, though they didn't mention Lincolns, hardly known in England in 1930. Styling had advanced somewhat by the time the Berliet arrived on the scene, so something had to be done to stress the warmed-over 1931 Cord-Chrysler hood and vee grille, rather than the boxy sedan body, with its mandatory, inelegant rear trunk. This particular idiom called for a long hood, which one didn't get with only 2 litres of four-cylinder engine. The copy precises and paraphrases Ford's interest in fuel taxes. Hence the adoption of valve-in-head motors by a firm who'd long been content with L-heads. The car offered nothing you couldn't get more cheaply on a Citroën or Renault – except, of course, rarity. Not that Berliet cared: they were already France's most successful makers of heavy trucks.

LINCOLN **Ford** Fordson

AIRCRAFT

NEW FORD DE LUXE FORDOR SALOON WITH SLIDING ROOF 24 H.P. £225 AT WORKS, MANCHESTER. (14.9 h.p. £5 extra)

Every riding and driving comfort you can desire

THE ENDURING beauty of the New Ford reflects the immense amount of trouble taken and money spent to build real and lasting value into this fine car. The lustre of elegant coachwork, built to give maximum safety, and rustless steel is matched by a degree of engineering skill and workmanship not to be found in any car at anything near the price.

It is one of the simplest cars ever built—easy to handle—responsive to the throttle—steady and safe at any speed. And it carries, as standard equipment, everything you need for your comfort.

Every detail of the New Ford has been designed to give you smooth, trouble-free and economical running during all the years of its long life.

Ask your nearest Ford dealer for a trial run.

NEW FORD PRICES

Tudor Saloon, 24 h.p.	. . .	£180
Touring Car ,,	. . .	£185
Standard Coupé ,,	. .	£185
Cabriolet ,,	. .	£210
3-window Fordor Saloon, 24 h.p.	. .	£210
De Luxe Touring Car ,,	. .	£225

All prices at works, Manchester. 14.9 h.p. £5 extra.

FORD MOTOR COMPANY LIMITED : LONDON AND MANCHESTER

La Société Française FORD offre à tout automobiliste la perfection mécanique réservée jusqu'ici à une élite restreinte :
Une 8 cylindres en V, moteur suspendu, silencieux et équilibré, puissance fiscale 21 CV. Boîte de vitesse synchronisée, deuxième vitesse silencieuse, freins puissants sur les quatre roues, amortisseurs hydrauliques à double réglage par thermostat. Nouvelle ligne longue, châssis surbaissé, carrosserie luxueusement aménagée. 130 Kms à l'heure en toute sécurité. Cette voiture constitue plus qu'un progrès, c'est une révolution.

Conduite intérieure.

32.900

8 cylindres en V

Société *Ford* Française

26.900
Conduite intérieure.

Si vous êtes fidèle à la 4 cylindres, essayez-la, elle vous étonnera. La nouvelle 4 cylindres FORD d'une puissance fiscale de 19 CV présente identiquement les mêmes perfectionnements mécaniques que la 8 cylindres. Pratique, durable, nerveuse, économique, elle est ce qu'a toujours été la FORD: imbattable. Mêmes carrosseries et mêmes modèles que la 8 cylindres, aussi spacieuse et aussi luxueuse qu'elle, la nouvelle 4 cylindres FORD représente une avance mécanique considérable.

même 4 cyl. *châssis*

France's effort to promote the new Fords in 1932 stresses price – all the amenities one gets on the four-cylinder model for only 26,900 francs, though by this time one is saving only two taxable horsepower a year by opting for 105 km/h (65 mph) instead of the vee-eight's sizzling 130 km/h (80 mph). In those times of depression, the cheapest two-door sedans are shown rather than the more attractive – and more expensive – cabriolets. There is a careful, almost Bellochian, "mention of virtues": the dampers, which were hydraulic, duly rate a mention. The brakes, mechanical and destined to stay so for another six seasons, are dismissed as "powerful", which they were not.

reserved their 1934 effort ("Listen for the Silence") for the home market, while Morris's rhyming, jingoistic "British Made for Empire Trade" would hardly have gone down with Belgians, who had their own colonial empire and wanted it to buy FNs, much less with Germans clamouring for more *Lebensraum*. Advertising tended to be a local affair.

When attempts were made to produce something different for foreigners, the result could backfire. Leonard Lord, the then head of Austin, was shrewd enough to recognize that "You Buy a Car, but You Invest in an Austin" was not a catchphrase likely to appeal in America, the land of planned obsolescence and yearly trade-ins, but his American importers did him a grave disservice with that prime *double entendre*: "Let's Take the Austin: The Car that is Always At Home". Some British campaigns were double-edged too: MG's habit of painting SAFETY FAST on the more dangerous, angled railroad bridges around the London area would never have been tolerated in the accident-conscious atmosphere of a later era.

It is too easy to generalize on the early promotional techniques of the industry. A quick glance at automobile advertising up to the early 1920s suggests a division into four obvious categories – "nuts and bolts", testimonials, illustrious clients, and competition successes. Illustrations, where used, were bald line or half-tone blocks of typical vehicles, with an occasional fling with the whole range to demonstrate comprehensive market coverage. Yet, stylized, elongated vehicles, depicted in the *art nouveau* mode, with typefaces to match, were used by such pedestrian French makers as La Buire and Turcat-Méry around 1921, even if the English text of the former's effort was at a loss for *le mot juste*. "The La Buire", it observed, "is not a car for which the manufacturers put forward sweeping claims, but its makers can speak emphatically on the two features that make the strongest appeal to the experienced motorist – reliability and durability." On a more elevated level were Edward S. Jordan's prentice efforts. It should be remembered that while the legendary *Somewhere West of Laramie* didn't happen until 1921, Jordan was using comparable themes – and equally good artwork – when he launched his first cars way back in 1916.

Jordan's masterpieces were, however, exceptions in a sea of depressing prose. "Nuts and bolts" often expressed themselves in terms of vital statistics and prices, the dreariness of the content being accentuated by the determination of the press department to extract the last cent's worth from every precious column-inch. Singer's 1938 range announcement started off promisingly enough with: "The first 'luxury' car at a popular price", but soon degenerated into a lengthy catalogue of features such as "synchromesh 4-speed and reverse gearbox" (which it ought to have had, anyway, by that time). "Powerful Head Lamps" was even more platitudinous, and the unhappy reader who had ventured so far had then to endure a similar recital in support of the parallel Nine and Ten.

Variations on this theme included essays in the technological and statistical. Ford's well-remembered Vanadium Steel campaign of 1907–08 had its echo as late as 1920 in Maxwell's "steels made to order", and a lot could be done with sales figures. "Sixty-eight per cent more than last year" could, after all, merely mean a comparison between the first fine careless rapture of a new range and the last declining weeks of the old. Even in November, 1936, SS were not above claiming that in the past month they had commanded nearly ninety per cent of the 20-hp taxation class in Britain. This was admirable psychology: horsepower tax counted for a lot at the time, the company had but recently discontinued their tax-dodging 16-hp variant, and in any case there were few readers who stopped to figure out who made the competing Twenties.

Euphoria played no part in the nuts-and-bolts school of thought. Nor

did the latter change much; the only difference between 1935 and 1905 is that more was taken for granted. To head one's copy "No Broken Axles", as did an obscure British importer in the Dark Ages, would have been unthinkable. Dependability – if it had to be plugged – was best plugged by stressing high trade-in values. Armstrong Siddeley and Packard made much of their factory-guaranteed used cars; the latter, indeed, compared theirs to a Verdi opera seen from a cheap seat in the gods – "He sees the same program, hears the same music". Austin proclaimed a car "as ready for its second or third year of service as its first, ... whose innate quality commands the highest price when you care to dispose of it".

Along with nuts-and-bolts came the testimonials, though in a less snobbish and exclusive age, such observations (on the correct letterhead, of course!) as "The Car has now gone Ten Thousand Miles Without A Single Involuntary Stop" were superfluous. Instead, famous racing personalities, such as George Eyston and Malcolm Campbell in Britain and Barney Oldfield in the United States, were called upon to endorse a model in the best cigarette-promotion style. As many of these eminent drivers doubled as motoring correspondents, their views were valid, even if their paeans were not necessarily the result of actual ownership. As for "illustrious clients", these were on their way out. There were fewer monarchs around in 1930 than in 1910, so the old maxim, "When in doubt, list your maharajahs", no longer obtained. Dying purveyors of chauffeur-driven carriages (Isotta Fraschini, Minerva) still adopted such methods, the latter company in an attempt to defend good taste against the march of American vulgarity. ("Whilst everything is carried out with the best possible workmanship, it is quiet and dignified, a car of genteel luxury unsullied by any Sir George Midas ostentation.") Even in 1928, Fiat were not averse to long lists of notables who drove their humble 509A, but the object of parading these Balkan princelings and African emirs was to stress global rather than snob appeal.

Consumer-report techniques mentioning the opposition by name were rare and generally provoked by extravagant claims. Such a war broke out between Chevrolet and Ford in 1934, after the latter had done well in stock-car racing. It had been far commoner in the first decade of the century. "Look what our machine beat at the local hill-climb" was, if confined for obvious reasons to the specialist press, a permitted gambit in the United States; and not only were the defeated victims identified, but their list prices, always higher than the victor's, were given! With an established sporting *marque* such as Bentley, who commemorated their third Le Mans win with a handsome booklet succinctly titled *Again*, competition themes remained acceptable. They were less acceptable in the case of minor-league events nobody had heard of, and the method had its pitfalls, especially in the prentice or declining years of a manufacturer's career. Too many of SS's early successes were in static *concours d'élégance*, while Austro-Daimler, once a proud name in the tougher hill-climbs and rallies, were down to Ruritanian beauty parades by 1933. The *reductio ad absurdum* of typographic laurels came after the Second World War, by which time motor sport was an accepted topic in newspapers and radio. Thus, victory in an ill-supported sub-category of a major international rally could spur copy-writers to a frenzied FIRST! (96-point bold). The reader was supposed to – and usually did – ignore the six-point qualification underneath, referring to Modified Production Touring Cars, 1,501 to 1,600 cc. More knowledgeable students, of course, were undeceived; they knew who was still running 1,600s, and who had recently overbored to 1,800 cc.

Factory-sponsored stunts were less common than of yore. There was less to prove. Top-gear marathons had still been popular in the 1920s,

Body by Fisher

It would greet you with a Smile • • •

If your motoring has become a sort of hum-drum transportation, there is that in the Buick which will bring back the zest of driving your first car.

Just to see the Buick is to realize how vivacious and new it is in its smart beauty. To drive it and ride in it but once is to recognize that it brings to modern motoring something new and all its own.

For there is a difference that goes beyond the gliding ride as only Buick gives it, beyond the matchless ease of superb performance and the convenience of automatic features. There seems to be the vigor and exuberance of youth in all that Buick does; and it is not difficult to imagine that, if it were human, it would always greet you with a smile.

You can take that kind of car to your heart—which perhaps explains the undying loyalty of Buick owners, and the even more wide-spread favor which Buick is winning today among motorists of all classes.

• B U I C K •

WHEN • BETTER • AUTOMOBILES • ARE • BUILT—BUICK • WILL • BUILD • THEM

The unattainable versus the only too attainable, thanks to time payments! This early Volkswagen advertisement (*left*) – off the front cover of *Motorschau* magazine – rates as state propaganda rather than advertising in the Western sense of the word. At the time it was published (July, 1938), the press had scarcely seen the car, and one wonders if the artist had, either: even allowing for poetic licence, both front and rear look very like the last batch of prototypes tried in 1937. The sedan's rear-seat headroom has been exaggerated, and the overhang at the tail is reminiscent of the contemporary 170H Mercedes-Benz. All the occupants of both cars look healthy, dedicated, and earnest: note also the "KdF" label (*Kraft durch Freude*, "Strength through Joy", the motto of Dr. Robert Ley's Nazi *Arbeitsfront*). *Volkswagen* was still only a generic term in 1938: everyone, including the foreign press, referred to the vehicle as a KdF-*Wagen*. General Motors (*right*) are also a little naughty, though 1935 Buicks really did look that way; where they overreached themselves was by showing the convertible with dual sidemounts when ninety per cent of the customers would buy the box-ier sedan, anyway. American euphoria is far more sybaritic than the German species, and jargon is much in evidence. "The gliding ride as only Buick gives it" is only another way of saying coil-spring independent front suspension, and "automatic features" in those days of synchromesh presumably refer to the company's addiction to starters operated by the gas pedal. The lady represents "the vigor and exuberance of youth" with no help from Buick, and if her father were the parsimonious sort and figured that she'd have to make do with a Chevrolet convertible, he'd have to think again. Chevrolet weren't making one in 1935.

113

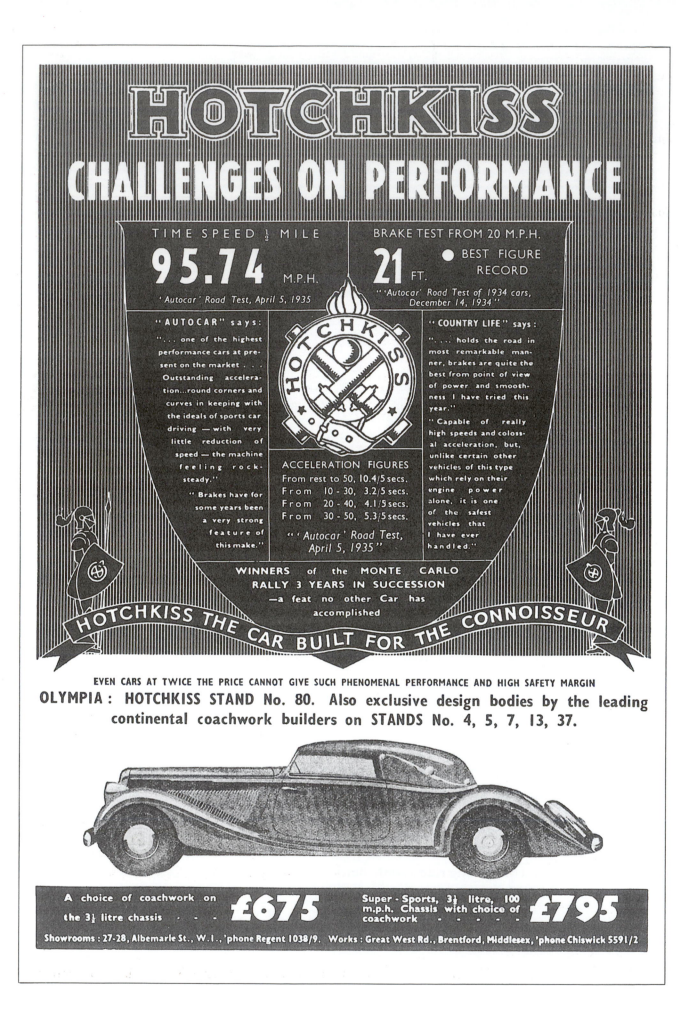

HOTCHKISS

CHALLENGES ON PERFORMANCE

TIME SPEED ½ MILE	BRAKE TEST FROM 20 M.P.H.
95.74 M.P.H.	**21** FT. ● BEST FIGURE RECORD
'Autocar' Road Test, April 5, 1935	"'Autocar' Road Test of 1934 cars, December 14, 1934"

"AUTOCAR" says:

"... one of the highest performance cars at present on the market ... Outstanding acceleration...round corners and curves in keeping with the ideals of sports car driving — with very little reduction of speed — the machine feeling rock-steady."

"Brakes have for some years been a very strong feature of this make."

ACCELERATION FIGURES
From rest to 50, 10.4/5 secs.
From 10 - 30, 3.2/5 secs.
From 20 - 40, 4.1/5 secs.
From 30 - 50, 5.3/5 secs.
"'Autocar' Road Test, April 5, 1935"

"COUNTRY LIFE" says:

"... holds the road in most remarkable manner, brakes are quite the best from point of view of power and smoothness I have tried this year."

"Capable of really high speeds and colossal acceleration, but, unlike certain other vehicles of this type which rely on their engine power alone, it is one of the safest vehicles that I have ever handled."

WINNERS of the **MONTE CARLO RALLY 3 YEARS IN SUCCESSION** —a feat no other Car has accomplished

HOTCHKISS THE CAR BUILT FOR THE CONNOISSEUR

EVEN CARS AT TWICE THE PRICE CANNOT GIVE SUCH PHENOMENAL PERFORMANCE AND HIGH SAFETY MARGIN

OLYMPIA : HOTCHKISS STAND No. 80. Also exclusive design bodies by the leading continental coachwork builders on STANDS No. 4, 5, 7, 13, 37.

A choice of coachwork on the 3½ litre chassis - - - **£675**	Super - Sports, 3½ litre, 100 m.p.h. Chassis with choice of coachwork - - - - **£795**

Showrooms : 27-28, Albemarle St., W.1., 'phone Regent 1038/9. Works : Great West Rd., Brentford, Middlesex, 'phone Chiswick 5591/2

British advertising for the 1935 French 3.5-litre Hotchkiss. Though well laid out, it is rather over-burdened with text: a hairy all-round performance counted for a lot when the Anglo-American Railton was plugging acceleration at the expense of contemporary railway publicity ("It's Quickest by Rail-ton" was a lovely riposte to "It's Quicker by Rail"). There was also a potential challenge to Bentley, which had been transformed, under Rolls-Royce ownership, into "The Silent Sports Car". And a Super-Sports at £795 ($3,980) cost little more than half the price of the Bentley. Elongation is carefully used to counterbalance the forward-mounted engine of the car; even with the illustrated Chapron cabriolet instead of the standard factory style, it was not quite as elegant as its picture.

the exploits of Violet Cordery and her various Invictas springing to mind. There were unofficial "saloon car hour" and "sports car hour" records to attack, and anyone who could put 100 miles or 160 km into sixty minutes on a stock model, using pump fuel, could rely on a few weeks of good publicity. Studebaker made capital out of their successes in the Gilmore-Yosemite Economy Run, and just before the war, Vauxhall sponsored a fuel consumption contest administered by their dealer-network, in which private owners were encouraged to compete. A brand-new feature could provoke a maker into something sensational. The slightly-tarnished image of Citroën's early *tractions* was undoubtedly rescued by the astonishing François Lecot, who set himself the task of driving one 400,000 km (248,560 miles) in twelve months, and won through, though nineteen hours a day must have been punishing for a fifty-eight-year-old. Less comprehensible was the exploit of the American Harry Hartz, who drove backwards around the United States in 1933 at the wheel of a specially adapted Plymouth. The theory behind this works-sponsored operation was that cars of the period had "better aerodynamics travelling backward than forward", whereas the forthcoming Airflow reversed the process. It all seems rather far-fetched.

The four advertising themes persisted – the maharajahs apart – throughout the 1930s and would, indeed, continue into the 1950s, leading one cynical observer to enquire why some advertisers consistently paid extra for colour when their copy was so totally uninspired. Jordan or no Jordan, Americans were so inured to nuts-and-bolts that Chrysler's first post-VJ campaign (plenty of colour, but not a car in sight) took them by surprise. Such a technique was, however, no novelty: Rolls-Royce had periodic spells of carlessness, and Duesenberg's best effort hit the roof in snobbery. A series run in the Depression years depicted a gentleman in his library (or Madame by her swimming-pool) with the simple caption: "He [or She] Drives a Duesenberg". Gladney Haig of Jowett, a past master of homespun, biblical prose, only bothered to show one of his company's stolid flat-twins when they had a new body style, which was seldom.

But new influences were at work – to stylize cars in picture, to emphasize the latest pain-killing techniques from every possible angle, and to inject an element of euphoria. This last would reach its zenith in such gems as Renault's *Ils S'Aimaient* brochure of the two lovers and their Floride (of course, it was a convertible), and Leyland's permissive "You Can Do It In An MG". The intent of Edward S. Jordan and his followers was, in effect, to tell the customer: "Buy This Car, and it'll be better than any dose of salts". Above all, they sought to blind him with science, using pure jargon (General Motors's Knee Action Suspension) or the camouflage of a routine improvement beneath a dramatic phrase. "Rhythmic Ride" was more euphonious than "Cushion Levelator", but they both added up to better shock absorbers than last year's.

Again, there was no real novelty. In pioneering days, automobile-oriented medicos of impeccable background could be persuaded to claim motoring as the panacea for everything – pure snake oil, in fact. Before 1914, Berliet and Hispano-Suiza had used very impressionistic colour-work to promote their luxury offerings, and in the immediate post-Armistice years, Delage scored a hit with a similar series: *"Rapide et Silencieuse, Elle Passe"*.

The motive in such cases was artistic. The cars were elegant, which is more than could be said for most cheap offerings of the 1920s. Thus, something had to be done to penetrate beneath that boxy skin and show that the new sedans had something euphoric to offer. A lay public neither knew nor comprehended the mysteries of overhead valves; and it could not be seduced by a dissertation on the relative merits of

Nuts and bolts at its most uninspired. Lots of facts – the gimmicks to cover up a lack of new ideas, or the money to finance them, and a leaf out of Rolls-Royce's book with the "two years' free periodical inspection". The illustration doesn't do justice to what was, in fact, a good-looking car, and not the Cord-and-cabbage-water idiom suggested. "Illustrated literature on application" hints at a shortage of dealers, whereas even in their declining years, Star had quite good agency coverage. Joseph Lisle, the founder, was violently opposed to volume production: "I would rather build one good car a day!" was one of his favourite sayings. In any case, in this specialist field advertising was really only a visual proof of survival, and when this plug for the 1931 range was published, the Star Motor Company had barely another eighteen months to go.

THE GLAMOROUS NEW 1939 PLYMOUTH! It is brilliantly new in styling, new in comfort, new in safety, new in economy. Experience the new smoothness of its improved Floating Power engine mountings, its easier-acting hydraulic brakes. Relax in the restful quiet of Plymouth's "radio studio" sound-proofing. This great new car is now on display at your nearby Plymouth dealer. See it today!

PLYMOUTH BUILDS GREAT CARS

PRICED WITH THE LOWEST

—

EASY TO BUY

The new Plymouth's low price and easy terms make it exceptionally easy to own. Your present car will probably represent a large proportion of Plymouth's low delivered price . . . the balance in surprisingly low monthly instalments. See your nearby Plymouth dealer today.

TUNE IN MAJOR BOWES' AMATEUR HOUR, C.B.S. NETWORK, THURSDAYS, 9 TO 10 P. M., E.S.T.

The United States versus Germany again
– or fun versus duty. Both advertisements
date from 1939, and the cars were both
six-cylinder family sedans, though the 2.5-
litre Adler was quite a lot more expensive,
being in the Humber or Buick class, so to
speak. The difference is one of outlook,
between the automobile as everybody's
friend, and the adjunct of a pan-Aryan
superman commuting from one *Autobahn's* end to another. The Plymouth's
background is Sunday-morning – drinks
on the lawn, with the dogs in attendance.
There's even a slight hint of poor relations calling, to judge from the Beverly
Hills colonial residence behind. By contrast, the Adler's crew are heading into a
symbolic nightmare worthy of Fritz Lang.
Such advertisements as Plymouth used
were generally accompanied by some
quasi-technical drawings, and folksy jargon dressing up commonplace features as
something special. Adler don't even mention that this is their prestige Six, with
conventional rear axle where the familiar
Trumpfs and Trumpf-Juniors (good for
thirty thousand a year) featured front-
wheel drive. It almost seems as if they
were trying to frighten the *Herrenvolk* off.
The 2.5-litre was one of the best
aerodynamic shapes of its time, good for
85 mph (130–135 km/h), despite a modest
flathead engine rated at 55 hp. Sales of a
mere five thousand in three seasons reflected a highish price: RM 5,750 (£300
or $1,500) was quite a lot to pay for a car
in Germany in 1939.

Adlerwagen sind Vorkämpfer des Fortschritts –

Abermals prägen die Adlerwerke einen neuen Begriff für Fahren –

Raumgröße – Wirtschaftlichkeit: ADLER

2,5 Liter   6 Zylinder   58 PS

expanding and contracting brakes. One has only to compare Maxwell's tedious 1920 discourse on steel with what Chrysler had to say of that marque's successor, the 1926 Model 70. "It spurts smoothly and easily ahead: it turns, it steers, it stops even as you think the thought. There's joy – new joy – in the lives of those who own and drive the new Chrysler Six."

The 70 might "respond to your will as if it were a part of you", but the accompanying photograph brought one back to earth. Hence, subsequent press campaigns used a stylized car shape which symbolized the Chrysler's undoubted virtues without showing such miseries as clumsy roof peaks and headlamps shaped like biscuit tins. Climbing ability was emphasized by tilting the printing block diagonally upwards. Others followed: Harry Ainsworth of Hotchkiss, only too aware that *le juste milieu's* appearance was mediocre, had artist Alexis Kow depict it in an elongated form, which sold a lot of cars and was cheaper than a restyle in the metal. Later on, Kow would perform the same service for the sleeve-valve Panhard, an individual machine but not always an elegant one. (His wife complemented his efforts by starting the fashion for parading with borzois at *concours d'élégance*.)

Artificially elongated hoods and speed streaks were complemented by the performing midgets, who were destined to outlive them. This family – which often included a dog – was truly international and consisted of approximately two-third scale humans, whose function was to stress the amount of room in any big sedan, be it American, French, or British. Their death was ultimately encompassed by the development of colour photography (real cars are always preferable) and by increasing emphasis on the station wagon, a vehicle dedicated to the indivisible load. Citroën's latter-day 2CV publicity was an outstanding example of this new realism.

Euphoria led inevitably to sex. Fairly antiseptic sex, be it said. Couples depicted in automobiles were usually married, or at any rate betrothed, and the object was to woo female drivers rather than to promote the sales of "bird traps". Not that the lady was often shown at the wheel; and hardly ever in Germany, where the sole concession to *Kinder, Kirche, Küche* was an austere housewife fetching her husband from the office in one of the tamer Mercedes Benz – never a 540K, which was a man's car. (The Germans were not averse to promoting the Luftwaffe, however: aircraft often featured in backgrounds.) As late as 1950, American makers tended to park Madame firmly in the passenger seat. Of that year's crop of sales literature, only Pontiac favoured women drivers. A few ladies were dotted about the catalogues of Buick, Nash, Oldsmobile, and Studebaker, but masculine domination was the order of the day. Oldsmobile's 1970 appeal to secretaries ("Wouldn't it be fun to have an escape machine") would have been unthinkable. As for allowing some of these ladies to be black …

Les girls were, nevertheless, firmly wooed. Austin added a dose of the old snake oil: "Many homes", proclaimed their catalogue, "are made healthy and happy because Mother and the youngsters are availing themselves of change of scene, fresh air, and sunshine." Lincoln carried the maternal instinct a step further with their 1937 Mother's Day advertisement. This was, of course, upper-class stuff; not many parents could afford to give Junior a $1,300 vee-twelve for his or her first car. Still, the mum who did "could wave goodbye to her children with a lighter heart – because they go in a Lincoln-Zephyr". At a more utilitarian level, Plymouths were said to appeal to housewives for their "immunity from squeaks and rattles, their freedom from frequent attention and adjustment, their sparing use of gasoline and oil … truly luxurious transportation at low cost". "Not a hair out of place" ran a choice piece of Buick copy showing a débutante stepping from her car, "thanks to Fisher's No-Draft Ventilation", though it wasn't specified

whether she drove herself to the ball. Nash went all out for feminine support in 1938, their "air conditioning" promoted by a glamorous blonde on the back seat in a fair degree of *déshabille* (for those times, that is). "Way below zero", ran the caption proudly, "and no wrap." Matrons were beguiled by a "life begins at 40" headline, but it meant 40 mph and went on to extol the virtues of the brand-new overdrive, one of a series of controls "literally made to order for flick-of-the-wrist driving".

Boy-meets-girl was an infrequent theme, though Dodge used an echo of *Laramie* ideas to promote one of their last roadsters. Snobbery, however, triumphed in this case. Our young couple were "individuals of standing whose personal belongings invariably are distinctive as well as correct".

If prestige counted most, value for money was an eminently permitted gambit. Nobody likes to spend money on fuel, and in 1938, Wolseley, as well as the modest Vauxhall and Standard, were talking in terms of low fuel consumption.

Standard presented their Eight as "the car built to beat the Budget", a reference to the recent tax increases and to their own preference for the long-stroke motor. In France the Simca-built Fiat 500 was credited with *l'appetit d'un oiseau* ("the appetite of a bird"), while during the Depression, Riley, with a sporting middle-class image, went even further: "Next Year will be a Year of Economy. It's Got To Be", though they made up for these Morris-like sentiments by reminding readers that their "car of economy" possessed "a standard of safety which no car lacking in experience of strenuous tests on road and track … can possibly offer you". Even Packard could ooze luxury now and then – what price "the rich luxury of genuine long wearing wool broadcloth smoothly contoured over deep hair cushions and oil tempered springs, tailored to the specifications of one of the world's leading orthopaedic surgeons"? Nevertheless, the main theme of the subsequent advertising campaign was a down-to-earth average annual repair bill of precisely $15.31.

Everything had, of course, to be *de luxe*. Stripped models sorted ill with euphoric techniques, and in any case, the public did not buy them. Morris's "hundred pound car" was the big sensation of 1931, but people still preferred to pay another £25 ($125) for chromium plate and a five-lamp lighting set. Auburn deliberately filled dealers' showrooms with "Salon" models loaded with extras; they sold better, and there was more profit on the deal. Much of the hyperbole in American advertising stemmed, in fact, from a determination to make the customer buy all the options which were never part of the package at the advertised price. Under the stripped-price system, almost everything was extra.

To illustrate the workings of the scheme, let us look at Nash's cheapest 1934 six-cylinder sedan at $695 (£139) ex-works Kenosha, Wisconsin. Assuming the customer lived near the factory and so was exempt from freight charges, the car he got for his money came with a single windshield wiper, no bumpers, and no spare wheel. Thus, "extras" essential to everyday motoring added a round $100 (£20) to the bill. Add such favourite gimmicks as radio, heater, dual sidemounts, clock, cigar lighter, and trumpet horns (most of them shown in the advertisement that had lured the prospect into the showroom), and the actual delivered price was pretty close to that quoted for the same factory's straight-eight. And while in theory you could drive away in a $695 Nash, "extras" were often compulsory. Every Studebaker President of the 1936 model run came complete with twin tail lamps, twin horns, and cigar lighters, but all these items were supplementary to the list price of $1,065 (£213). This policy would reach ludicrous proportions on Lincolns of the early 1950s, available only with "optional extra" automatic. This was a matter of prestige; as yet, the Ford Motor Com-

One that eluded the Holy See. Everyone knows the story of the 1934 Fiat Balilla advertisement featuring the lady whose skirt showed too much. Vatican pressure led to some minor but significant "fashion changes", though the uncensored original hangs in Fiat's factory museum to this day. Intriguingly, she was not the only Fast Lady to help promote the latest in baby Fiats. This delectable piece of publicity appears on the back cover of one of *Rivista*'s 1925 issues and is plugging the company's first true cheap miniature, the 990-cc overhead-camshaft 509, made until 1929. The thoughtful trick (confined, incidentally, to home-market cars) of recording the type designation in huge nickel-plated script on the radiator core saves the copy writer a lot of trouble, while the lady's anatomy helps to conceal the awful truth: the 509 was quite as boxy as any of the Chryslers later hymned — and camouflaged — by McKnight Kauffer. In any case, the birth of a new Fiat was (and is) a national event in Italy. To launch the 509, the company laid on a brand-new hire purchase (time payment) scheme. Why use a super model to promote something so utilitarian? One must remember that precious few Italians could afford cars (or glossy magazines, for that matter) in 1925, and probably not more than one in every two hundred citizens actually owned even a humble Fiat. Thus, "Song without Words" styles worthy of Rolls-Royce or Duesenberg in the thirties would not be impossibly out of place.

Reginette

Artist's licence. The 1934 Panhard Six as it looked in the metal and as redrawn by that publicity-virtuoso Alexis Kow. Not even clever two-toning could make a beauty of this stolid sedan with its wood artillery wheels (you could have bolt-on wires, but not a lot of customers did), while the split-pillar *panoramique* wind-shield merely highlighted the thickness of the stock 1931-type pillars and led to some curious reflections. The hood was long, even on the smaller six-cylinder models, but the Kow advertisement gives the impression of the rare 8DS straight-eight, a 5-litre affair made only in small numbers.

pany's own automatic was not ready, so to suggest dependence on General Motors's Hydramatic (which Lincoln used) would have involved loss of face. The time would eventually come when the customer paid extra for "low-cost" manual gearboxes, because demand for these was down to a trickle!

This may explain why utilitarian themes vanished from American advertising. Only Willys, in financial trouble and struggling to make ends meet with a 2.2-litre four at $495 (£99), could describe this dreary little creature as "the car that helps buy many things the family needs". After a brief, euphoric skirmish with "the spirit of youth", they were back on the economy trail in 1942, with "a straight-from-the-shoulder message to everyone who weighs the worth of a dollar" – not to mention a 25 mpg thirst on the eve of fuel rationing.

Blinding the customers with science was a safe gambit – especially if this suggested that in some way the manufacturer cared. The nasty umbrella-handle hand-brake was there to clear the floor of projections and accommodate three people in front, but it was promoted as a safety feature. So was Chrysler's unloved transmission brake, which was said to leave the drums on the wheels free for regular duties of retardation. Buick's radio was "specially designed for the acoustical properties of the Buick body". Nobody was averse to making a virtue out of necessity. The first post-war Crosley minicars were finished in "a light metallic gray-blue reminiscent of the wings of the mourning dove, reflected in the sunlight", but what the company did not add was that Powel Crosley was trying to save dimes by eliminating colour choices.

Fancy names concealed mundane features. Chrysler's "safety signal speedometers" of 1939 were what they purported to be, with different colour zones for different speed ranges. It was, however, naughty of Hudson to pass their warning lights off as "teleflash gauges". Press departments rediscovered – and murdered – classical Greek, while an assortment of euphemisms camouflaged the soggy independent suspensions of the period. Ford, of course, left these latter alone, preferring to defend their old transverse-leaf set-up as "long, slow action springs of multi-leaf design", but General Motors had "knee action", while Hudson boosted "Axle Flex".

Nor were such euphemisms fully explained. The 1939 Hudsons came with a choice of Handishift or Selective Automatic Shift. Also present were Automatically Controlled Wing Ventilation, Triple Seal Oil Cushioned Clutches, and Hydraulic Hill Hold, meaning, respectively, a new type of ventipane, the same old wet-plate clutch the company had been using for twenty years, and a sprag incorporated in the transmission to prevent the car running back on hills. Dodge, noted for a commonsense outlook, had "air styled headlamps" (attached to the radiator grille) in 1935. When their engine was enlarged and given a stiffer crankshaft in 1942, it acquired "Power Flow", while 1949's raised compression ratio promoted it to a "Getaway". Either way it was the indestructible old 230, which had roots going back to the beginning of our period, and which was destined to survive in light trucks until 1966. Hudson's "Miracle H-Power" (1951) had nothing to do with nuclear fission; they had merely thrown in an extra carburettor.

As for transmissions, no holds were barred. "Automatics" were not always automatic: Hudson's 1939 effort was an orthodox manual with clutchless change. Dog-Greek terms were used for the real thing: General Motors had Hydramatic and Dynaflow, Packard's contribution was Ultramatic, and Ford progressed from Liquimatic to Fordomatic. The streamline craze of 1934 taxed the vocabularies of press agents to the limit. Chrysler's Airflow was logical enough, and Hupmobile made "aerodynamic" a trademark. Pontiac called their 1935 turret top models Silver Streaks after a famous diesel train of the period; Nashes were "Speedstreams" or "Aeroforms". After all this, it is a little disappointing to discover that the limits of Hudson's "symphonic styling", a novelty of 1941, were some new ideas in two-toning.

Anything could be a virtue. In 1931, Chrysler offered "the driving pleasure of two distinctly different high gears," on their short-lived four-speed transmission, but two years later, the driver of a Reo had "nothing to do at all", since his car "automatically selects and engages the right gear for every road condition". Nowhere was it mentioned that on this "greatest invention since the self-starter" a range-change called for use of the clutch. By contrast, Vauxhall's "a perfect gear change every time" (synchromesh) sounds modest and unassuming. Ford, who were slow off the mark with hardtops in 1950, made up for it in deathless prose. The Lincoln Capri was "a brilliant gem in rich velvet, with wide, sweeping picturescape windows". "What a glorious experience," continued the catalogue, "it is to lounge in the abundant luxury of the Cosmopolitan Capri." And yet this car, unlike its General Motors and Chrysler rivals, was little more than a two-door sedan with a vinyl top.

The advertisers were making a determined onslaught on that most powerful of opponents, marque loyalty, which was certainly a force to be reckoned with.

The young SS firm, recording a banner year for their new Jaguars in 1936, claimed that one buyer in three was a repeat customer. If such a claim could not be made, the "experienced motorist" was a useful runner-up. Under Rootes control, Humber had changed their image substantially between 1929 and 1932, so a useful selling point was that "every third Humber owner you meet was a motorist before the War". Further, 87.5 per cent of such owners had had at least six previous cars; hardly surprising, when Humber prices started at £395 ($1,975), or what one paid for three Baby Austins in those days. The same year, the front-wheel-drive Cord, on its way out, claimed "extraordinary owner allegiance"; the advanced new transmission arrangements "spoiled them for other cars". Alas! Cord were doomed to disappointment; after a miserable performance (335 units sold), the company put the marque into mothballs for three years.

If advertising was used to woo new customers, the old ones were strengthened in their loyalty by a tightening up of dealer networks. Good agents meant good sales.

In early days, there were few garages, and responsible dealers were fewer still. Even in 1910, good dealer networks were confined to the United States and perhaps France. Elsewhere, except in the case of the most popular makes, the customer bought from the factory or from a distributing agent in the nearest big city. Exclusive agencies were not understood. "Any Make of Car Supplied" was a common catchphrase in Britain, and a situation from which neither trader nor client profited. The former received a lower discount, and the latter had to wait longer (and pay more) for replacement parts. Not that this latter service was necessarily inefficient; in 1910, Hotchkiss's London importers claimed that any part could be obtained from Paris within twenty-four hours. Ford apart, few manufacturers bothered much about the other agencies their outlets held. In the writer's small home town the Morris dealer not only ignored Wolseley (that franchise stayed where it had been in pre-Nuffield days), but also handled Talbot, already a Rootes subsidiary.

Dealer networks, of course, varied with the size of the company. In 1931, Chrysler had ten thousand dealers in the United States alone, irrespective of those who handled other makes in the group. In the same year, Fiat, for all their international ramifications, ran to a mere sixteen hundred, of whom some five hundred were in Italy. At the other end of the spectrum, Rolls Royce (who referred strictly to "retailers") had twenty-six in the United Kingdom, plus a small number of

sub-retailers in more prosperous territories. Really small specialist makers – Frazer Nash in Britain, for instance – invariably sold direct.

Good dealers were imperative. They also tended to see the writing on the wall long before the public became aware of an impending bankruptcy. There were extensive defections during Hupmobile's declining years, and the demise of the Clyno in 1929 was undoubtedly accelerated by the withdrawal of Rootes support in the previous year.

Thus, young firms were often at a disadvantage, especially in the 1930s. If SS inherited some support through their previous connections (as the Swallow Coachbuilding Company) with Britain's important Henly chain, and Volkswagen inherited the Adler network after that company abdicated from cars, the American Austin firm was reduced to some very odd outlets, including at least one small-town grocer. Worse sufferers were foreign imports, since all too often the domestic opposition had snapped up the better garages.

To marque loyalty, then, had to be added dealer loyalty. A make could survive a technical or even an economic volte-face at the factory – more folk than would willingly admit it remained loyal to Vauxhall after the General Motors takeover, the cheap and nasty Cadet coinciding with a fall in their incomes after 1929. But what marque loyalty could not survive was poor service, and the record of the writer's family between 1916 and 1940 is an interesting illustration of the rewards a good dealer could expect. Of thirty-two cars and trucks owned during the period, all but eight were Morrises, and all but six were Nuffield products, the sons following the father's choice of make. At least two of these cars – one from the late 1920s and another bought in 1933 – were absolute shockers, and were rapidly passed on, but their failings were promptly dealt with by the dealer. It is also significant that, since leaving that neighbourhood, no member of the family has shown any great bias towards the Oxonian marque.

Servicing underwent one major change – the provision of factory exchange units. These had long been available in the United States but did not reach Europe until the middle thirties. Hitherto, a defective component – unless it could be replaced under warranty – had to be repaired, and often, it had to be sent away for repair to specialists. Such phrases as "recent rebore" are all too common in used-car advertisements of the 1930s and early 1940s. The new system was cheaper – and quicker.

Also a growing habit was the purchase of cars "on time". By 1928, fifty-eight per cent of all new models sold in the United States were the subject of hire-purchase agreements, even if Henry Ford disapproved, instructing his salesmen to stress the advantages to everyone of cash on the nail. By the 1930s, the official British figure was fifty per cent, but informed opinion suggested that seventy-five was nearer the truth; "putting it on the book" was still someting one didn't discuss in polite circles. Manufacturers often ran their own self-financed hire-purchase schemes; this went for all Britain's Big Six, for Fiat in Italy, and for Opel and DKW in Germany. Citroën even went so far as to assign separate chassis serials for cars so supplied, though this "security check" did not last long.

As war approached, euphoria was riding the crest of the wave. Americans knew what was coming, but one catches the spirit of a favourite post-war theme – "away from it all". In 1940, Lincoln invited their customers to take a trip into the hills of Vermont, "where many a road ... leaves the village abruptly and points towards the mountainside. It bends and twists, following the clear, stony brook beside it. Each turn brings its own little world of greenness, until an upland finds you in a whole swirl of intimate mountains". "If your car doesn't mind them", continued the travelogue, "roads like this bring their rewards." Needless to say, the Lincoln-Zephyr revelled in rural

Euphoria triumphant. By 1940–41, the rest of the world was at war, but the American car industry was enjoying a boom, and it no longer bothered with technical asides. The inserts in the 1940 Nash advertisement illustrated, in theory, an overhead-valve engine, independent front suspension (which curiously never went under that name), and their familiar "air conditioning", which wasn't quite what they said, though advanced enough for its time. In fact, they just showed cars in suitably escapist settings. The elongators have, as usual, been at work: the 1940 Nash was neither as long nor as wide as the artwork suggests, and the cheap flathead on the 117-inch (2.97 m) wheelbase was almost boxy, especially when fitted with the alternative trunkback style not usually depicted in Nash publicity. One must expect a plug for the company's by-now traditional fuel bed-seats, but if you think "automatic overtake" means "automatic overdrive", you are wrong – it's the action of disengaging overdrive for maximum acceleration.

Lincoln were escapologists in the Busby Berkeley class: this 1941 Zephyr advertisement is almost brutally practical by their prevailing standards. "Glider ride" is somehow linked with twelve cylinders, something only Lincoln still offered; it was also an excellent cover-up for the hard fact that not even a long wheelbase and low build could really cancel out the weaknesses of Ford's all-transverse suspension. They were not afraid to assign a gender (masculine) to their car, hydraulic brakes get a heavy plug (people were so used to Ford's mechanicals that they'd forgotten this was the new system's third year). With war and rationing only a few months away, much was made of the Zephyr's modest fuel consumption, one of its few unassailable virtues. Oddly, the two-speed rear axle (an option by now peculiar to Ford Motor Company products) was ignored. Maybe they felt that the Lincoln's 20 mpg (14 lit/100) were good enough in their own right.

MORE FUN PER GALLON

You can't measure it by slide-rule or calipers—but you'll know in your heart that the matchless thrill you get from a Lincoln-Zephyr is what you've always wanted in a motor car!

For you need only glimpse the breath-taking beauty of a Lincoln-Zephyr—feel the live horse-power of its 12 eager cylinders—relax in the cradled comfort of its magic *glider-ride*, to realize why owners everywhere get more fun per gallon in this "only-car-of-its-kind".

And that's just as true, whether you drive a Lincoln-Zephyr for business and social rounds, or to make the whole sports map of America, from Northern pine to Southern palm, your playground.

Created by Lincoln engineers and built to exacting standards in the renowned Lincoln precision plant, this new Lincoln-Zephyr is rugged, able, modern through and through, with he-car capacity to "take it." Different in design,

different in basic construction, different in engine—its operating-thrift is astonishing!

Unit body-and-frame construction in closed body types puts steel-welded safety around you. Sound insulation hushes road noise and traffic roar. Doors open by push-button. Tops on convertible models are electrically operated. The famous new *glider-ride* with scientific springing and larger shock absorbers fairly skims you over rough spots. Husky hydraulic brakes give you smooth, dependable, equalized stopping power.

Won't you visit your Lincoln dealer soon and arrange for a demonstration of the new 1941 Lincoln-Zephyr? Learn for yourself the pleasure of owning a car that gives you *more fun per gallon*—to look at, to ride in, to drive!

LINCOLN MOTOR CAR DIVISION, FORD MOTOR COMPANY
Builders also of the Lincoln-Continental, Cabriolet and Coupe; the Lincoln-Custom, Sedan and Limousine.

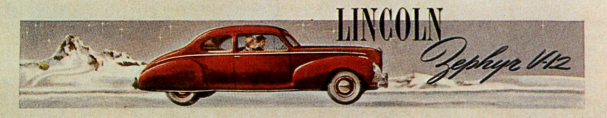

LINCOLN
Zephyr V-12

EXCLUSIVE with Nash . . . manifold-sealed engine pick-up of 15 to 50 MPH in 12.9 seconds, high gear; also, an economy class-winner in the Gilmore-Yosemite Run (21.25 miles to the gallon).

BADLAND ROADS are smoothed by the Arrow-Flight combination of individual coil springs in front—super shock absorbers controlling long, synchronous springs in back.

Night Flight

THERE'S MAGIC in the air tonight. Fleecy clouds sail high above . . . and your road is a ribbon of glistening moonlight.

Keen and crisp is the whistling wind. But inside your Nash you're sitting snug and coatless, in the never-changing June of the "Weather Eye".

Far into the satiny night your Sealed Beam lights cut an arc of glareless day. Yawning bumps cast shadows ahead—but the line of your lights never wavers, so level is the Arrow-Flight ride.

You sit there . . . fascinated by the ease you take turns, curves, hills, without slewing or slacking . . . hands barely touching the wheel . . . eyes never leaving the road.

And as you ghost through sleeping town after town, in the soft, soundless stride of the Fourth Speed Forward, only the speedometer shares your secret.

Then suddenly ahead, a tail-light blinks. But a gentle nudge of your toe, and the new Nash Automatic Overtake zooms you by in a terrific burst of sprinting power.

On and on you go, up starlit hill, down darkened dale . . . your heart singing with excitement . . . your Nash a silver phantom under the great white moon.

Sure, you can make up that convertible bed in back if you want to break the spell . . . but chances are that when the sleepy world awakes, you'll be whistling over breakfast, three states away.

• • •

It's only fair to tell you this. You don't need the thrill of a moonlight night. In 60 minutes, anywhere, a 1940 Nash will make you unhappy 'til you own it.

Luckily, it costs so little you'll jump at the chance to trade in your old car. See your Nash dealer today and find out!

GREAT DAYS AHEAD with Nash's convertible bed, and automatic "Weather Eye" for conditioned-air comfort, cleanliness, on trips. Nation-wide service by 1800 Nash dealers.

Again... IT'S THAT NEW **NASH**

mountaineering. One may hope that some jaded businessman, dreaming of his summer vacation, went out at this juncture and bought himself such a car.

They were still at it during the war years, promising "Someday, a rendezvous with the clouds". Euphoria had taken over.

Peculiar to the United States in our period – and indeed for many years to come – was radio advertising. The American technique has always centred around the sponsored programme rather than the interspersed commercial, and American citizens learnt to associate Major Bowes's Celebrity Hour with Chrysler, the André Kostelanetz orchestra with Pontiac, and old-time dancing with Ford (Old Henry was militant in his hatred of jazz). While such programmes were perhaps mildly educational, the commercials were frenetic. For Hudson, in 1934, there was no refined euphoria, no faint hint of "Getting One's Girl". The crescendo came in the best circus-barker style: "On the water, it's aqua-planing. In the air, it's aero-planing. But on land, Hot Diggety Dog, IT'S TERRAPLANING." How different from the ghost-story voice of the 1960s, adjuring one to enjoy "four-on-the floor", Posi-Traction, and the other delights of Pontiac's hairy GTO – "with care".

Political propaganda with the fresh air and fun of a 1939 Opel Cabrio-Limousine, or what can the *Herrenvolk* be looking at? Just to make sure that no official secrets percolate outside, the artist has used a stylized Junkers Ju.52 instead of the Ju.88 he could already have drawn. The doughty old 52 had, after all, been around since 1930 and was still employed by a number of European airlines.

Auf den Erfahrungen der in den letzten 3 Jahren zehntausendfach bewährten Konstruktion aufbauend, sind dem OLYMPIA die neuesten Fortschritte der Technik dienstbar gemacht worden. Der neue Hochleistungsmotor, die beachtliche Vergrößerung des Innenraumes und der Spur, die bessere Sicht lassen ihn noch mehr als bisher die höchsten Anforderungen für Straßen und Autobahn, für Stadtverkehr und große Reisen spielend meistern . . . Altbewährtes und fortschrittlich Neues wurde so im OPEL OLYMPIA zu hoher Wirksamkeit vereint.

EIN NEUER OPEL OLYMPIA

INDEX

Page numbers in italics indicates illustrations